KV-513-641

Hertfordshire
COUNTY COUNCIL
Community Information

1 2 APR 2003

1 7 MAR 2004
1 3 OCT 2006

12 | 11

Please renew/return this item by the last date shown.

So that your telephone call is charged at local rate, please call the numbers as set out below:

	From Area codes 01923 or 020:	From the rest of Herts:
Renewals:	01923 471373	01438 737373
Enquiries:	01923 471333	01438 737333
Minicom:	01923 471599	01438 737599

L32 **www.hertsdirect.org**

The American West

Robin May
&
G. A. Embleton

Focus on History

ALMARK PUBLISHING CO. LTD., LONDON

First published—November 1973

551
ISBN 0 85524 105 5 (hard cover edition)
ISBN 0 85524 106 5 (paper covered edition)

Printed in Great Britain by
Vale Press Ltd., Mitcham, Surrey CR4 4HR
for the publishers
Almark Publishing Co. Ltd.,
49 Malden Way, New Malden,
Surrey, KT3 6EA
England.

Introduction

THERE was nothing romantic about the 'real' American West except the scenery, despite every effort of film and television companies, and generations of authors, to prove otherwise. Yet there was something grander about the discovery, exploration and settlement of the American West than mere romance. It was an epic. In fact, it remains *the* American epic, capturing the imagination of millions around the world, and not just in the United States.

Guns, guts and barbed wire helped tame the West after a struggle that lasted more than 350 years, though the main concern of this book is the Wild West in the usual sense of the phrase, a period roughly from 1865 to the 1890s.

There were many 'Wests'. Usually the first one is taken to mean the time when would-be settlers poured across the Appalachians into Kentucky's 'dark and bloody ground' and beyond from the 1770s onwards. However, the 'West' of this book is the most usual one, the trans-Mississippi West.

White men first entered this West in 1540 at a time when there were perhaps a million Indians in what is now the United States, and countless millions of buffalo. The intruders were Spaniards under Hernando de Soto, heading north from Mexico in search of mythical cities of gold. Though this ill-fated expedition found no golden cities, it reached what became Kansas to the north and Oklahoma and Texas to the east.

The Spaniards did not at first follow up their early expeditions, and by the time Spain began to build missions, villages and ranches from California to Florida in the early 18th century, the fierce tribes of the Southwest had become brilliant horsemen as a result of Hernando de Soto's expedition leaving behind some horses which became the fore-runners of the great herds of wild plains horses. The Comanches, the Lords of the South Plains, played havoc with the Texas missions in the 1750s and, when the Spanish settlers retaliated, routed them. French arms helped the Indians, the French having penetrated south from Canada.

Only in California, where a succession of fine priests worked, did Spain's colonial dreams succeed. The Southwest was in a state of perpetual turbulence, especially from raiding Apaches, and not for the last time the order went out: 'Exterminate the Apaches!'

Before this task could be attempted, Spain's whole attention was drawn to Europe. Over some 40 years Britain gained Canada from France, lost her American Colonies, and fought the Revolutionary and Napoleonic Wars, and in all these except the first—the Seven Years War, known in America as the French and Indian War—Spain was deeply involved. Her Southwestern frontier became a backwater. So when the first Americans reached the West in 1804, Spain's political influence, California and the extreme Southwest apart, counted for very little.

3

Yet in certain ways that influence remains to this day—in place names, religion, dress, traditions and language. And, as we shall see, the cattle Spain brought to the New World were to be the ancestors of that mean, hard-hided, history-making beast, the Texas Longhorn.

With the first American expedition, led by Captain Meriwether Lewis and Lieutenant William Clark, the story of the American West, wild, woolly and otherwise, really begins. The French had regained ownership of Louisiana in 1800, which was then not merely the area of the present State, but the whole trans-Mississippi Valley from the river to the Rockies. In 1803, President Jefferson bought this huge territory from France for just over $11 million, though legal tangles finally doubled that sum. It was cheap at the price, for overnight the young United States doubled in size.

Into this unknown land went Lewis and Clark to explore it as widely as possible and to find out if a trans-continental water route existed. Much of the expedition was by water, but no such route was found, yet the journey was a true success, opening American eyes to a new heritage. It was also a human success. Of the 33 who set out from winter quarters in an Indian village in Dakota in 1805, all reached the Pacific and returned safely, including Sacajawea, the Indian guide and interpreter, her infant son, and York, Clark's black slave, whose prowess and popularity with Indian squaws was a notable feature of the trip. Another, more important, feature was that Lewis and Clark got on admirably with most of the Indians they encountered. The presence of an Indian girl helped, but the leaders set civilised standards. It was a peaceful beginning to the violent, bloody years which were to follow.

CONTENTS

1: The Mountain Men

THEY were the toughest white men who ever roamed the West. Hard cases like Jesse James and Billy the Kid seem pale by comparison with them. They have come down to us as the Mountain Men, though they blazed trails over the Plains and the deserts as well as across the Rockies and other great ranges.

Their main task was to trap beaver, whose fur was then fashionable in the East and in Europe, especially for hats. They were mostly Americans of British descent, though there were others in the trade, including Britons, Mexicans and French Canadians. They flourished from around 1810 to the 1840s, by which time silk hats had replaced beaver ones and the trade was finished, but by then these wild men, who

were almost white Indians, had crossed and re-crossed almost all the West.

The first of the Mountain Men is often said to have been John Colter, who had been a member of the Lewis and Clark expedition. He was the first white man to see the spectacular Tetons of Wyoming and the wonders of Yellowstone, and his career was typical of the Mountain Men who followed, though even Jedediah Smith and Jim Bridger, the most famous of them, never had to endure the 'race against death' which befell the rugged Colter at the hands of the Blackfeet.

Captured by a large war party one autumn day in 1808 in what is now Montana after a fellow trapper was killed by the Indians, he was given a punishment worthy of an old enemy of the tribe. He was stripped naked, marched a short distance away, then told to save himself.

Scores of braves armed with hunting spears at once came after him, as he started in the direction of the Madison River, six miles away. Though thorns and prickly pear tore at his feet, he outstripped all his pursuers except one, who threw his spear, but stumbled. The spear broke as it fell at Colter's feet. He grabbed it and killed the Indian, then ran on.

Reaching the Madison, he dived in, swam to some drifting brushwood and hid beneath it as the first Blackfeet came into view. The Indians searched up and down the bank for him as he hid in the icy water, then they gave up with howls of rage.

But Colter's ordeal had only just begun. He survived a week-long nightmare journey, enduring freezing nights and burning days, his feet reduced to bloody lumps of flesh and his food mainly roots, until at last he reached his camp on the Big Horn. Filthy, bearded and covered in blood, he must have looked an awesome sight even to the Mountain Men who greeted him, but he soon recovered. His kind had a way of surviving.

Even the businessmen who organised the fur trade were larger than life. John Jacob Astor, founder of the famous family of Anglo-American millionaires, rose from being a poor German immigrant, through trips into Indian country back East carrying stinking skins on his back, to fabulous riches. In the 1790s, he found that beaver skin could be bought off an Indian for a piece of bright, cheap cloth and sold for a 900% profit, £2 in the currency of the time. Such were the huge possibilities of the fur trade, which dated back to the earliest days of the French settlers in Canada.

Astor, faced with competition from two great Canadian companies, the Hudson's Bay and the North West Company (which amalgamated in 1821), made his first fur fortune in the East. Later he hoped to base a western empire on Astoria, to be built an the mouth of the Columbia River on the Pacific Coast. A chain of similar trading posts and forts was to stretch to the Missouri, but Astoria failed from bad management, bad luck and other factors, so Astor concentrated on his American Fur Company in the heart of the West.

The sufferers from the grandiose schemes of Astor and others were the Indians, who were usually underpaid and softened up for more by rot-gut liquor. But to Astor business was business: he once sold half a million muskrat skins in a day. Shrewdly, he sold out in the 1830s, rightly sensing the end of the beaver trade, and concentrated on property.

The other fur trade kings were the Spaniard, Manuel Lisa, unlikeable, hot-tempered, but with a genius for organisation, and the Americans, William Ashley and Andrew Henry. They often led their men personally, though trappers like Smith and Bridger were born leaders themselves. Lisa had the Missouri trade under his control until he died in 1820. No charmer, he could yet talk to hundreds of hostile Sioux, and if he had to fight, he fought.

Then in 1822, came an advertisement by Ashley and Henry in the *Missouri Gazette* for "Enterprising young men", which attracted a legendary list of applicants, among them Smith, Thomas 'Brokenhand' Fitzpatrick, William Sublette and young Bridger, who must have got someone to read the advertisement, as he could neither read nor write. The era of the Mountain Men was about to reach its climax.

Ashley and Henry had combined to combat British influence in what Americans now considered their Northwest by forming the Rocky Mountain Fur Company, but Indians were the main problem on their first expeditions. By 1824, Henry had had enough and returned to mining, reading and playing the violin back East, but Ashley led his men on many rugged expeditions. Some Mountain Men hired out their services, others worked alone or in small groups after their time with Ashley ended. They fought Indians and most of them married them. Toughness was their trademark, but they were not all wild. Jedediah Smith, who pioneered the route to California, leading a party across the terrible deserts of southern Nevada and eastern California and surviving starvation and thirst, was sober and religious. He endured even worse desert treks, a clash with a grizzly that scarred him for life, and fights with Indians, before being killed by a Comanche lance at the age of 31 in 1831.

8

Jedediah Smith, Mountain Man (Denver Public Library. Western History Department).

LEFT: A trapper in his winter gear of blanket coat and fur cap.

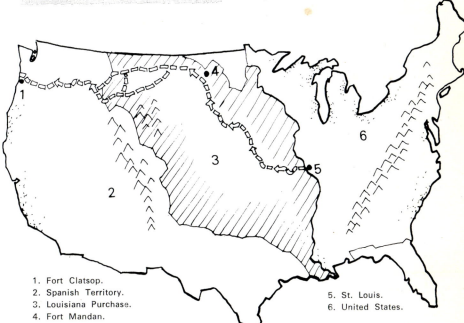

1. Fort Clatsop.
2. Spanish Territory.
3. Louisiana Purchase.
4. Fort Mandan.

5. St. Louis.
6. United States.

Trail of Lewis and Clark, the expedition that opened up the West.

Jim Bridger, Mountain Man, Indian fighter, scout, guide and teller of tall tales. (Kansas State Historical Society).

Jim Bridger, the illiterate, could speak French and ten Indian languages, and was the first white man to taste the bitter waters of the Great Salt Lake. He, too, survived countless Indian fights, but unlike 'Diah' Smith, lived on 40 years after the trade in furs had collapsed, working as a guide, scout and trader, and telling tall stories, the tallest of which were sometimes true. He knew the West better than any white man before or since, one of his memory aids being that he regularly looked back on the trail, as well as sideways and forwards. But then he was full of useful tips, such as getting rid of vermin from his buckskins by dry-cleaning them over an ant-hill.

Perhaps the toughest Mountain Man of all was Old Hugh Glass who—so the story goes—was deserted by two companions after he had come off a poor second best in an encounter with a grizzly. Furiously he set off on a 200 mile crawl to avenge himself, living on berries and the bodies of dead buffalo calves. He caught up with the first deserter, who, according to most accounts, was young Jim Bridger, though Bridger's finest biographer, J. Cecil Alter, will have none of it. Glass forgave the youth, whoever he was, but continued searching for the other false friend. Finally he found him, but to his disgust could not touch him as he had joined the Army.

The Canadians, too, had their heroes, especially Pete Skene Ogden of the Hudson's Bay Company, who was the equal of any American Mountain Man. The Company's bosses in the Northwest, the gigantic John McLoughlin and his dynamic chief, Sir George Simpson, were finally beaten by international politics when the Oregon Treaty of 1846 gave the Oregon country to the USA and established the 49th Parallel as the boundary line.

Every summer Mountain Men would gather at a previously chosen rendezvous camp, often in the Rockies, a scheme which was originally Ashley's. At these annual sprees, they talked, drank, gambled, traded skins, raced their horses, fixed themselves up with Indian wives, and often fought pitched battles in horseplay and savage earnest. At night, laughter and drunken shouts and songs filled the camp. The fighting tended to take place by day.

Agents from the fur companies travelled from their headquarters to the camps, bringing money, goods, weapons and tools to exchange for skins. Most of the Mountain Men were such habitual gamblers that they were quite prepared to risk their entire earnings in a single session. But then few of them were the settling kind. Money meant almost little to them as it did to the Indians.

It was a raw scene, and often barbaric, yet it must also have been hugely enjoyable. But the meetings got smaller and smaller in the 30s as the fur trade began to collapse, and men like Old Bill Williams and young Kit Carson and the rest had to start thinking of other suitable occupations. Guiding wagon trains or exploration parties was not, of course, the same as a season's trapping alone or with a few choice companions hundreds of miles from such oases of 'civilisation' as Bent's Fort or Fort Laramie, but it was better than settling down. Ashley was the exception; he settled for politics.

Over-trapping had almost wiped out the beaver from many Western streams, but the fur trade continued to flourish in Canada, as it does to this day, well over a century since the high noon of the American Mountain Man.

Strangely, modern film-makers, hynpotised perhaps by six-gun lore, have not made much of the Mountain Man in his fringed buckskin suit, and with his muzzle-loading rifle and powder horn. Fortunately, Washington Irving wrote about them, but the classic book on them was written by a young British ex-army officer, Frederick Ruxton, whose wanderlust led him to the Mountain Men's West when the fur trade was practically over, but when many of the most colourful characters were still active—and as loquacious as ever. His *Life in the Far West*, first serialised in Blackwood's Magazine in 1848, with a modern edition published in 1951 (University of Oklahoma Press) is our ultimate source today of how they lived, spoke and thought. All their splendidly boastful exuberance is contained in the reported words of one of them, a Negro called Moses (Black) Harris, who told an admirer:

> '. . . I've trapped on Platte and Arkansa, and away up on Missoura and Yaller Stone; I've trapped on Columbia, on Lewis Fork, and Green River . . . I've fout the 'Blackfoot' (d--d bad Injuns they are); I've 'raised the hair' of more than one Apach . . . I've trapped in Heav'n, in airth, and h--!'

12

2: Wagons Westwards

THE streets of Independence, Missouri, were thronged with horses, oxen mules and every variety of men: well-fed store keepers, Spanish traders gamblers, Indians, Mountain Men. In this booming town even the creaking of wagons and crack of whips were drowned by the sound of hammers on anvils, as blacksmiths worked night and day preparing wagons for the 2,000 mile journey over plains and mountains to Oregon.

Such was Independence in the 1840s, when three great trails started from there, not only the fabulous Oregon Trail, but the ones to California and Santa Fe as well. The ordinary men, women and children who braved them were the truest heroes of the American West, facing every hazard from starvation to Indian attacks in search of a promised land. They were America on the move, and those that survived their often terrible journey put down roots to settle the land over which Mountain Men had merely passed.

Though the Oregon Trail was not the first, for the mainly trading route to Santa Fe had been in operation since the 1820s, it must be dealt with first for it was *the* trail. Oregon's beautiful and fertile Willamette Valley was the paradise the emigrants sought. Thousands of them headed towards it in the 1840s in covered wagons whose wheels dug ruts so deep that some of them can be seen to this day. It was the greatest recorded trek in history, and one of the most severe tests of human endurance, especially for the first parties who were often hopelessly ill-equipped for their journey.

Rumours of the earthly paradise in the Williamette Valley had been circulating for years. Much of the actual trail had been blazed by the trappers and traders of the Mountain Man era, but few did more to spark off mass emigration than a tall, black-bearded Methodist missionary named Jason Lee. After building a mission in the valley in 1834, around which some settlers gathered, he gave a series of thrilling lectures about Oregon when he returned East in 1838-39, which electrified everyone who heard them. Oregon Fever was in the air. Ironically, when he had first reached the valley, he had been given every assistance by John McLoughlin of the Hudson's Bay Company, which was to be ousted from Oregon by the treaty of 1846, along with all British influence.

After small-scale crossings in 1841-42, the first great wagon train set out in 1843, 200 families strong in 120 wagons. It set the pattern for later crossings, having an elected captain, Peter Burnett, and a Mountain Man, John Gantt, as guide.

Emigrants set out every spring to make sure that Oregon was reached by winter and that there was enough fresh pasturage for the animals. A wagon train was a moving town, containing not only hundreds of families but men skilled in every trade and its share of adventurers and criminals. The wagons were covered farm wagons, smaller than the freighters of the Santa Fe Trail. Prosperous families would often have several wagons.

Most of the emigrants were hardy, restless farming families. At first, after leaving Independence, or one of the other Missouri frontier towns, the going was easy through the low hills of eastern Kansas. There was a magic moment forty miles from Independence where the Santa Fe Trail branched off and a sign read Road to Oregon. Soon they were following the Platte across the Plains, where they began to pass the carcasses of dead horses and cattle, shallow graves and piles of cast-off possessions. There were huge herds of buffalo still, which often held the travellers up, and they cooked over dried buffalo dung. Diarrhoea and nappy rash were constant companions on the journey, which grew steadily dustier, but the main peril of the trail was cholera, a killer far more deadly than the Indians who, whatever the legends, rarely attacked wagon trains, not only because they were moving fortresses, but because Indians had little reason as yet to hate the whites.

If a wagon broke down, its occupants were often left behind—if they were lucky, with a few friends. Delay might be fatal for Oregon had to be reached by winter, as did California by the few that broke off to follow the California Trail. The mass movement to California dated from the Gold Rush of 1849.

Yet it was the California Trail which proved the dangers of delay, for the Donner Party of 1846 failed to reach its destination, and, after appalling hardships, was trapped in the Sierra Nevada Mountains. In the nightmare that followed seven men and a boy died in one makeshift camp and were eaten, some while their families looked on.

The average wagon train on the Oregon Trail travelled two miles an hour and twelve miles a day. At first, horses were used, but later, oxen were found to be far better for such hard conditions. A highspot was the arrival at Fort Laramie, a time for replenishing supplies, mending wagons and, for the wives, washing clothes.

The next stop was Fort Bridger, 394 miles on, and over 1,000 miles from Independence. True, the backbone of the Continent had been passed by now by going through South Pass, only 7,500 feet up in the Rockies, but the price was exhaustion and gaunt oxen, then beyond the Pass, an 'unmeasureable and sterile surface', as a traveller described it. Those who took a short cut to miss Fort Bridger endured 50 waterless miles as a reward.

From Fort Hall the journey got worse. The first emigrants tried giving up their wagons and taking to horses, crossing turbulent rivers on rafts, or boats generously lent by the Hudson's Bay Company. But later, the terrors or the Snake and the Columbia were avoided when land routes were found, though many died finding them. Every known variation of climate assaulted the pioneers, or so it must have seemed to them, and every sort of terrain had to be endured. Perhaps as few

Above: Wagon train crossing the Smoky Hill River in 1867. (Kansas State Historical Society).

as 10,000 actually reached Oregon between 1841 and 1846, but it was not the numbers that counted; it was the fact that they were there to settle, and by their mere presence ensure, that the Northwest explored by Lewis and Clark and the Mountain Men remained American. And, more important, the idea of the West and westward expansion became an American dream more firmly than ever before.

While traffic on the Oregon Trail was reaching its peak, events further east were conspiring to start a route which was unique. This was the Mormon Trail. Most people headed West for land or, later, gold, a few for sheer adventure, or to escape the law, but the Mormons simply sought religious freedom, and even those least sympathetic to them could hardly deny their indomitable spirit.

Their original leader, Joseph Smith, had founded his Church of Jesus Christ of Latter Day Saints in New York State in 1830, producing a Book of Mormon as its bible. Driven from their first home in Ohio because the neighbours objected—a pattern which kept recurring—the industrious but narrow community of Saints reached Jackson County, Missouri, where their very success, and the fact that they were anti-slavery in a pro-slavery area, provoked riots in 1838. They fled to Illinois and founded Nauvoo on the Mississippi.

Smith himself destroyed his flourishing settlement by arrogantly considering himself above local law, then, in 1843, by announcing that polygamy was permitted, which split his own people and aroused 'Gentiles' around Nauvoo to fury. He was murdered by a mob, but Mormonism was saved when a masterful 43-year-old, Brigham Young, became the new leader. In mid-winter he led his people to temporary safety at Camp of Israel and the following winter to Winter Quarters in Nebraska.

15

In Spring, 1847, a strictly disciplined advance party set out under Young and reached Salt Lake Valley. 'This is the place', announced Young and the next day his people were planting crops.

What seemed like a miracle to the fervent Mormons saved the next Spring's crops, on which the thousands of Mormons now streaming to Salt Lake would depend. Millions of grasshoppers of a breed called Mormon Crickets descended on the wheat and started devouring it, but when all seemed lost seagulls appeared and ate the grasshoppers. The seagull remains an honoured bird in Salt Lake City.

Through the Mormons' genius for attracting recruits, many from the industrial slums of Britain, converts were soon flocking across the Plains. Brigham Young's inspired idea for 1849 was to introduce handcarts to carry baggage of up to 500lbs, and over a four year period 3,000 Saints pulled the carts all the way to Salt Lake City, averaging 30 miles a day, which was more than twice as fast as most ox-teams could manage.

Even in their new home, where they 'made the desert bloom', Mormons could not escape hostility, polygamy seeming infinitely more shocking to the average American than other aspects of the Wild West. Besides, the Mormons were so different. They actually tried to co-exist with their Indians, even after Indian attacks. And they were not interested in gold. When the world seemed to be flocking to California, Brigham Young said that gold was for paving streets.

Young was appointed Territorial Governor of Utah in 1850 by President Fillmore. Tensions went on for years between Gentiles, who considered him a tyrant in charge of a theocracy, and Mormons who resented outside interference. The Mormon cause was not helped when, in 1857, with President Buchanan declaring Utah to be in a state of open rebellion, Mormons encouraged and helped a band of Utes wipe out some admittedly troublesome emigrants in a manner somewhat similar to the nightmarish massacre of Britons at Cawnpore in India the same year.

Young, who lived until 1877, was in no way responsible for this. This extraordinary, fanatical genius, the maker of Utah, left over $2 million to 17 wives and 56 children. In 1896, Utah, with polygamy abolished officially at least, became a state, and Mormon and Gentile were finally reconciled.

If the Mormon Trail was unique, the Santa Fe Trail was certainly unusual because, unlike other routes, famous and little-known, it was almost entirely given over to trade. From the early 1820s, American traders and trappers used the trail, caravans carrying goods to Santa Fe and returning with skins and precious metals. At the start of the war with Mexico in 1846, one caravan of 400 wagons was on the trail, worth nearly $2 million. Later, raiding Comanches and Kiowas turned the Santa Fe into a trail of blood. The first flood of settlers into Texas in the 1820s and 30s used no one route as they scrambled out of the South, sometimes writing GTT on their old homes—Gone to Texas—in case anyone wondered where they had suddenly vanished to.

Above: An emigrant train of Mormons en route to Salt Lake City, 1867. (Utah State Historical Society).

Right: Brigham Young, aged about 65. (Utah State Historical Society)

The much larger-than-life early history of Anglo-American Texas began in 1821, the year Mexico broke free from Spain. That year, 300 American families were given permission to settle in Texas, their leader being a 28-year-old, flute-playing lawyer, Stephen Austin, as quiet as the traditional Texan has been flamboyant.

From the first the settlers, with their different culture and traditions, riled their distant rulers in Mexico City. The Government tried to curb them, even abolishing slavery, the colonists having brought their slaves from the South with them. Whatever ultra-liberals may say in praise of Mexican motives, the abolition of slavery by rulers whose treatment of their own peasants varied from bad to infamous, was probably aimed at the colonists' cotton economy. Austin got the Government to agree that the children of slaves should be free at 14, and that slaves could not be sold after coming to Texas, and a crisis was averted.

In 1833, an army officer named Santa Anna seized power in Mexico and became President, and at first many of the Americans, now 20,000 strong, half favoured him as an able man who might grant them privileges and give them good government. But the proud, cruel, elegant new dictator, so refined that he had a silver chamber pot carried on his campaigns, proved no friend of the Americans of Texas, who prepared to rebel. The year of reckoning was 1836, with the American Texans outnumbered the local Mexicans by about 30,000 to 7,000.

With such an advantage, the Texan rebels were at first successful, but soon Santa Anna was moving north, his Spanish pride and his ruthlessness making him a dangerous enemy. Meanwhile, at Washington-on-the-Brazos Texas declared its independence and its army was put under the command of Sam Houston.

This extraordinary man had not fought since the Creek War of 1814. He had been Governor of Tennessee and a Congressman, had lived with the Cherokees—he is one of the only known examples of a Texan who genuinely loved Indians—and he had a formidable reputation as a drinker. Such was the attractive, brilliant man destined to be first President of Texas.

But now Santa Anna was closing in on a San Antonio mission-turned fortress called the Alamo. Heroism is an unfashionable word today, but by any standards the defenders of the Alamo from February 23 to March 6, 1836, were as heroic as their fate was tragic. A fiery young lawyer, William B. Travis, the legendary Davy Crockett, like Houston from Tennessee, and Jim Bowie of lethal knife fame, together with about 180 others after a few reinforcements arrived, held off about 4,000 Mexicans. Travis supplied an immortal message, a battle cry as much as a plea for help:

'TO THE PEOPLE OF TEXAS AND ALL AMERICANS IN THE WORLD . . . I shall never surrender or retreat . . . If this call is neglected, I am determined to sustain myself as long as possible and die like a soldier who never forgets what is due to his own honour and that of his country—VICTORY OR DEATH'.

Death it was to be for all that valiant garrison and for hundreds of Mexicans. But Texas had been given time, time to survive. Fifteen women and children came out of the Alamo alive, and now there

Above: The Bray photograph of Sam Houston, Texan, Statesman and Injun-lover. (Library of Congress)

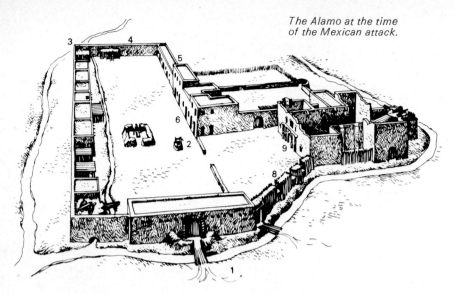

The Alamo at the time of the Mexican attack.

1. Barracks and main gate.
2. Well.
3. Position of Travis.
4. North wall breached here.

5. Main barracks.
6. The hospital.
8. Davy Crockett and his men positioned here.
9. The chapel where Jim Bowie died.

followed another massacre when over 300 Texans, who had surrendered to a Mexican force at Goliad, at Santa Anna's orders were murdered to a man.

Now there was only Houston's army of 800 left, and it was in full retreat. But at San Jacinto the over-confident Santa Anna was surprised by the Texans, who went into battle shouting: 'Remember the Alamo!' The action lasted 20 minutes or less and what exactly happened remains a mystery, except for the basic facts: only nine Texans killed, Santa Anna taken prisoner, and about 600 of his men dead. It was April, and by September Sam Houston had been elected President.

It took him until 1845, with a period out of office, to achieve his main ambition, the annexation of Texas by the United States. The difficulty had been the cancer that was eating away at the Union— slavery. The last thing many Northerners wanted was another slave state. When the Civil War began in 1861, Texas joined the Confederacy, but Houston, who had been in turn President, Senator and finally Governor of Texas, supported the Union and had to retire from public life.

ABOVE: *Sodbusters in Custer County, Nebraska, 1892. BELOW: Main Street, Nebraska City, c. 1865. (Nebraska State Historical Society).*

ABOVE: Sodbusters in Indian Territory. On the left are Cherokee girls, like the rest, dressed in their best clothes. (Western History Collections, University of Oklahoma Library).

OPPOSITE, TOP: A party of travellers under attack—the loss of their horses could be a fatal disaster. OPPOSITE, BOTTOM: Typical travellers on the trail.

The so-called Texas House—two separate rooms or sets of rooms with a connecting roofed-in area. It was sometimes walled in on the windy side.

But meanwhile the whole pattern of the Southwest had been changed by an aggressive, expansionist war by the United States against Mexico (1846-48), which gave the Americans most of Arizona and New Mexico—they got the rest in 1853—and also the greatest prize of all, California. Nine days before the peace treaty was signed in February 1848, a small yellow object caught the eye of an employee of a rich Swiss-born Californian landowner named 'Colonel' John Sutter. Fate had decreed that the Golden West was to be America.

3: Gold Rush

'Gold! Gold! Gold from the American River!'
THE inhabitants of the small Californian town of San Francisco saw a wild-eyed, bearded man rushing down the street and shouting with a bottle of gold dust in his hands. Or so the story goes. Cynics suggested that Sam Brannan, Mormon and future Vigilante leader, merely showed the bottle to anyone he saw in the street. Whatever the truth of the events that day in May, 1848, the result is not in dispute. By June, 'all were off to the mines. some on carts, some on horses, some on crutches, and one went in a litter,' as one eye-witness later recalled.

And that was only the start, the local gold rush. The world-wide stampede to the Californian goldfields happened in 1849, the year of the 'Forty-Niners'.

It was the biggest bonanza of them all, sweeping whole continents with gold fever. And it created a pattern which kept repeating itself. First came the rumour of a strike—in America or elsewhere—then, because travel was becoming easier, the rush began. Ships were deserted. Office boys in the eastern states, in London, in Europe, left their desks and headed for the docks. Good men and bad men set out for the goldfields. Many never arrived, many more never found gold, but a few found wealth past imagining. Such was the power of gold fever that some of those who took part in the Californian Gold Rush in their teens were to be found heading for the Klondike in 1898.

RIGHT: Panning for gold near Virginia City, Montana, 1871. (National Archives).

The Forty-Niners found California securely American. The area, which had been the only remarkable Spanish attempt at colonisation in North America, was too remote from Mexico City to withstand slick annexation by the Americans in 1847, the main object of their war against Mexico. Gold was discovered on January 24, 1848, just over a week before California officially became American. The peace treaty gave the United States her Far West, Oregon Territory already being hers, at a cost of only $15 million. Five years later she paid another $10 million for southern Arizona and New Mexico. And by then, California may have already produced $250 million worth of gold.

The first strike of all happened during the building of a saw mill on the property of a Swiss emigrant, John Sutter. The work as we have seen, was being supervised by his head carpenter, James Marshall, and it was he who first saw gold. Sutter and Marshall swore all hands to secrecy, but Sam Brannan, riding over to Sutter's spread after hearing some rumours, could not be expected to keep the secret—and didn't!

At first, the stampede was a small one, being confined merely to every ship's crew in San Francisco harbour and almost every man in the area, as well as most of the women and children. California, despite the California Trail, which had never been used so much as the route to Oregon, had only around 14,000 whites at the time, and many of them were of Spanish descent and not quite so smitten with gold fever as the Anglo-Americans. So that first rush, in which finds included lumps of pure gold of over 25 lbs, was confined to perhaps 1,000 people.

The news spread fast, and ships sailed from Hawaii direct, around Cape Horn from the eastern states, and from Britain and elsewhere. Expeditions set out from Mexico. Others, grossly ill-equipped for the journey, surged across the Plains, where many died from exhaustion or Indian arrows. The survivors reached Eldorado. Some took the most rugged route of all, across the fever-ridden swamps of the isthmus of Panama on the principle that it was a short cut. It was also a killer.

There was never anything like that first spring and summer for the lucky ones at the goldfields. Even the weather seemed bent on providing its blessing on an already lovely area. True, hunting for food drew a man away from his main purpose in life, but then the high summer sun would shrink streams and there the miners would see deposits of gravel containing gold for the picking. One new arrival struck it rich to the tune of 45 ounces of gold the day he arrived. It was small wonder that men would pan for gold in a freezing river under a burning sun for hours on end when the pickings, in the early days at least, were so good.

The biggest boom year of all was 1852, when $81 million worth of gold was found—and California's population had soared to a quarter of a million. By 1900, over $1,000 million worth had been found.

Yet comparatively few made fortunes, even in the early days before mining gold became an industry. The unfortunate Sutter, with squatters invading and camping out on his land—much of which

Gold rush days in California, from a Currier and Ives print. (Library of Congress).

the Supreme Court later ruled was not his—was almost ruined. Though some actual miners made—and kept—fortunes, the richest people as a group were the traders and businessmen who followed the prospectors to California. One Italian, Domenico Ghirardelli, started on the millionaire's trail by selling chocolates and sweets to the miners. Other, more conventional, candidates for riches were merchants and financial wizards like Leland Stanford, Collis Huntingdon and the De Youngs, dubbed 'grocers' by jealous rivals, which doubtless failed to ruffle their spirits as they made their millions.

The ultimate losers in the Gold Rush were California's Indians, 100,000 of them, who were 'in the way'. They were mostly backward and un-warlike, with none of the genius for fighting that the Plains Indians possessed. By 1860, there were only about 30,000 of them left alive after the rest had been murdered, or died of white diseases or from harsh enslavement. Gang-rapes of Indian girls became, as William Brandon has written in *The American Heritage Book of Indians*, 'so common that even the white press took cognizance.' Even after mass extermination ceased and the survivors had been confined to arid reservations, atrocities occurred. In 1871, ranchers in the Sacramento Valley, finding a steer which had been wounded by Indians, followed their trail, found them in a cave and killed 30. In the cave, an old-timer recalled, were some Indian children. Kingsley could not bear to kill these children with his 56-Spencer rifle as it 'tore them up so'. He used his ·38 calibre Smith and Wesson revolver instead. Such was the dark side of the rise of the Golden State.

Not that Indians were the only sufferers. Few Wests were wilder than California's in Gold Rush days, and San Francisco, transformed from a sleepy little town of some 800 people, became a violent jungle of tents, shacks and hastily erected buildings, ruled by thieves and killers. How law and order—of a sort—came to the city is told in chapter Five.

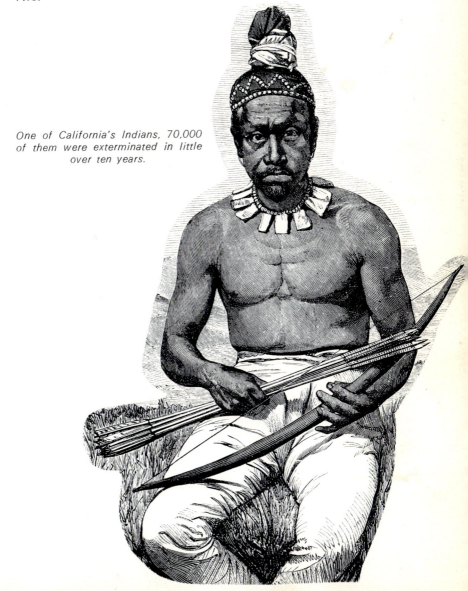

One of California's Indians, 70,000 of them were exterminated in little over ten years.

California's was *the* Gold Rush, and before passing on to other legendary spots like Virginia City, Deadwood and the Klondike, its importance must be stressed, for it was far more than a get-rich-quick spree. It was one of the key events in American history, making her suddenly and fantastically rich, helping to populate and open up the West, and setting her on her rocket-like rise to World Power. Gold fever in this case spelt national prosperity, and California has been basking in the glow from it ever since. Not for nothing is she called the Golden State.

Meanwhile, the mining boom moved inland. The most sensational find, always referred to as the Big Bonanza, was the Comstock Lode, an immensely rich vein of silver, much of it spangled with gold. The original strike was in 1859, but it was the 1873 silver strike which made the nearby boom town of Virginia City, Nevada, the most fabulous mining centre in the West, with a reputation that reached far beyond the United States.

The Comstock was named for a claim jumper, Henry Comstock, who was bought out before anyone realised how rich a find the lode was. It was producing around $16½ million a year, but by 1872, it seemed to be played out. Yet two years later, with the latest equipment installed, it produced $38 million. San Francisco, 200 miles away to the west, where much of the money went, started to sprout millionaires. By 1900, when Virginia City's population had shrunk to less than a tenth of the 30,000 who lived and worked there in its matchless heyday, the mines had produced over half a billion dollars worth of silver and gold.

One splendid feature of the Comstock was that the richest men in town were not 'grocers' but miners, who had started work swinging picks and shovels. A quarter of Irishmen, John Mackay, James Fair, Jack O'Brien and James Flood, were the leading Mining Kings, though before 1872 they were mere princes.

Mackay was the emperor of them. He had arrived penniless in 1859 with O'Brien. Approaching the already booming town, O'Brien had thrown away their last half dollar for luck and said: 'Let's enter like gentlemen!' They sauntered in to make their fortunes.

Mackay was down one of his mines at 6 a.m. every morning. That sort of dedication, plus the most up-to-date methods of mining, made Virginia City as efficient as it was world-famous. The local millionaires included J. P. Jones, who later became a senator. It was said of him that he counted his dollars by millions and that he had about five times as many millions as he had fingers and toes.

The key to the success of a Bonanza King was that after his initial find, he did not lose all his money in traditional ways: gambling, bad luck, lack of business know-how, women, robbery, lead-poisoning or drink, or combinations of any of them. A man like Mackay, who saw the level of work descend from four feet below the surface to 1,500 feet, was a geologist and an engineer as much as a miner. Mackay, the self-taught expert, could simply look at a sample of ore and tell the worth of the silver in it almost as accurately as an assayer. He would try any new machinery. It was all worlds away from the wild and woolly lynch-happy, claim-jumping days of 1849. At the Comstock,

Prospectors, with the impedimenta of their calling: pans, shovels and mules. (US National Archives).

miners flocked in to work regular hours for the Bonanza Kings, and though the silver finally ran out, Virginia City never endured the humiliation of becoming a complete Ghost Town, and today has become a major tourist attraction. Fortunately, for posterity a local newspaper-man, Dan De Quille, wrote a classic about the Comstock called—what else?—*The Big Bonanza*.

Nearly every Western territory and state had its own gold or silver rush, often several times over. Colorado, where Oscar Wilde once lectured to startled miners in Leadville, was a major mining area. Prospectors trekked northwest to the goldfields of Montana, a major cause of Red Cloud's War which, as we shall see, the Indians won. And it was a gold rush into the sacred Black Hills of the Sioux which led to Custer's Last Stand. As for Tombstone, the most famous of Arizona's mining towns, it owed its existence to the discovery by a prospector named Ed Schieffelin of a fabulous silver lode. The date was 1877 and the Apaches were by no means subdued. When Schieffelin told a friend he was off to prospect for stones, meaning quartz specimens, he was told: 'The only stone you'll find is your tombstone.' He later gave his diggings their legendary name.

As for the innumerable Lost Mines of the West, the Lost Dutchman, the Lost Adams, the Lost Breyfogle and the rest, hunting for their missing treasures remains a popular American pastime. Today's hunters are armed with electronic locators and study geology. Not for them the spectator sport of looking at Ghost Towns. They head for the deserts and the hills, sometimes risking everything from hunger and thirst to—in the case of the Lost Dutchman in the Superstition Mountains of Arizona—a mad marksman who is said to guard its secret. Looking for that mine two men at least have been beheaded, one as late as 1947. Such is the lure of gold.

The last major outbreak of gold fever resulted in the toughest trail of them all, the Trail of '98. The Klondike story belongs to Canada and the USA, though men from every Continent helped make it the epic it was. Some gold had been found on the last frontier—Alaska and Canada's Yukon Territory—before the great strike of 1896 occurred, on August 17 at Bonanza Creek, a tributary of the Klondike River.

Klondike stampedes at Lake Bennett, 1897/8, waiting for the ice to break before going downstream to Dawson. Note the boat builders in the background. (The Commissioner, Royal Canadian Mounted Police).

The lucky men were an American, George Carmack, and two Indians, Skookum Joe and Tagish Charley. They had been tipped off by Robert Henderson, a Canadian prospector who had just found a little gold himself.

The three struck it rich beyond a miner's dreams. Gold lay like a giant cheese sandwich between slabs of rock, and the small community of prospectors in the area were soon hurrying to the spot.

The Klondike was so far from civilisation that at first the outside world knew nothing of the strike. Though a detachment of Mounties arrived to keep order—a rare occurrence in a mining area—it was not until the winter was over that the news broke.

During that winter fortunes had been made and lost in Dawson, the local boom village, and gold rapidly became less valuable than salt. Henderson, still regarded by some today as the finder of the gold, had no part in the jubilation as he failed to strike it rich, then or later. Plenty did, and the following July two boatloads of Bonanza Kings reached Seattle and San Francisco, having sailed down the Yukon with every piece of luggage and every box and jar on the boats filled with gold. The world promptly went mad with a disease called by the papers Klondicitis.

A stampede started at once, most of the stampeders having no idea of what they were in for or where they were going. Some were frozen in for the winter in overcrowded boats on the Yukon River. Others endured nightmarish journeys overland. Those who made it by these routes found the Gold Rush over when they finally arrived.

There was only one feasible way—north by sea to Alaska, landing at Skagway, then trekking across two terrifying passes, the White and the Chilkoot, and on into the Klondike down the Yukon at its narrowest and most lethal. Home-made craft were used, but only when the ice broke.

In Dawson, now a fast-growing town, 'The Lion of the Yukon', Superintendent Sam Steele of the Mounties, was in charge. He issued strict orders that no one could enter the Klondike without a year's food supply, and had the two passes guarded to enforce the rule, which saved the Klondike from starvation.

However, many failed to get clear of the American town of Skagway where a very respectable-looking criminal named 'Soapy' Smith had the whole place in his pocket. He had acquired his odd nickname back in Colorado where he convinced gullible miners that the five dollar shaving soap sticks he sold might have dollars under their wrappers. The first stick always had a hundred dollar bill: nearly all the rest were—soap.

Few could pass through Skagway without falling into the hands of Soapy's gang. He controlled the town, the Law, the carriers on the passes and the routes to them. As taking a year's supplies to the top meant several journeys, Soapy and his boys made a killing. To add to the misery, too many prospectors were woefully ill-equipped for the near-arctic, mountainous conditions.

Dawson's population shot up to 40,000. It was lively, but law-

The NWMP Post on the Chilkoot Pass in 1898. Soapy Smith's gang did not get beyond this point. (The Commissioner, Royal Canadian Mounted Police).

abiding, and Steele's men kept Soapy's gang out. The flood of Stampeders arrived in the summer of '98, when 30,000 people in 7,000 boats came down the Yukon after the ice broke. By spring, '99, every creek had been staked, and every store-keeper in Dawson was chuckling, along with a few lucky prospectors. The next year, when the actual rush was over, £4 million worth of gold was extracted from the Klondike.

By then Smith was dead, the townspeople having risen against him, led by a brave man named Frank Reid who was killed himself. Soapy's gang escaped lynching, but not jail, and the non-stop sound of six-guns, which had characterised his reign of terror, ceased. In Dawson in '98 there had been not a single murder.

Dawson City in 1899 abounded in business opportunities for those able to resist the lure of gold. There were no price ceilings in the Klondike. Salt was literally worth its weight in gold. (The Commissioner, Royal Canadian Mounted Police).

As for George Carmack, he died rich, and Tagish Charley prospered until he was drowned when drunk. Skookum Joe, rich as he was, went on looking for gold till he died. So died poor Henderson, who was finally given a small pension by the Canadian Government.

Today, mining in the Yukon and Alaska is a technical business and the Stampede, like other gold rushes, seems a crazy, marvellous epic. Marvellous is too weak a word to describe the men and the women, too, who braved the Klondike trail. Most gold-seekers, even the greediest, had something of the true adventurer about them, but this was particularly so of the men of '98, as Pierre Berton so movingly describes in his definitive *Klondike.* Many who found nothing were proud simply to have reached their goal. They recalled it all their lives as the greatest time they had known, and they lived in the belief that nothing could now be impossible for them.

4: Cowboy

IN the summer of 1865, thousands of Texans, defeated in the Civil War, were making their way home. Many of them were cowboys and ranchers and they returned to find their ranches in ruins and hundreds of thousands of unbranded cattle running wild. There had been cowboys in America long before the Civil War had broken out in 1861: the word was in use in the late 18th century. There had been cattle drives before the war. Large and small herds had been driven from Texas to New Orleans, and some had gone westwards to California, others north to Missouri over the Shawnee Trail. But the cattle trade was still in its infancy and the cowboy was not yet the national figure he was soon to become.

The ranchers set to work to repair their property and round up stock. There was not much of a market for it locally, but in the north and east steers were said to be worth 50 dollars a head. Texas cattle were not today's pedigree specimens, but longhorns, now an extinct species except for a few bred as museum pieces of the range. The longhorns were the mean, wild descendants of the cattle brought to the Southwest by the original Spanish settlers and their hides were as tough as their natures, so tough that a joke went round about the rattler that bit a longhorn and died of lockjaw.

The first major drive out of Texas happened in 1866 and was not towards Kansas or Missouri but northwest towards the mining camps of Colorado. It was led by an adventurous 30-year-old, Charlie Goodnight, a superb rider with a sense of direction like an Indian's. He was a crack shot who had scouted during the war with the Texas Rangers.

Goodnight teamed up with 54-year-old Oliver Loving and, as the direct route was swarming with hostile Kiowas and Comanches, they decided to head west via New Mexico before swinging north.

They set off with 18 cowboys—or drovers as they were usually called in the early days—and 2,000 longhorns, and they nearly came to grief at the outset while crossing 80 waterless miles. By the third day out the longhorns were almost out of control, and, when the Pecos River was reached, the half-crazed beasts plunged in and were soon trampling on each other and getting stuck in quicksands. Goodnight got them through, sold some of his stock to the agent of some starving Navajos, then hurried back to Texas to collect more cattle, while Loving headed up the trail to Colorado.

Meeting again in New Mexico, the two established their new Goodnight-Loving Trail to the mining camps. Loving was later killed by a Comanche arrow, but Goodnight lived on until 1929, having become a handsome old patriarch and one of the greatest of all cattle kings, also one of the few who got on with Indians.

Meanwhile drovers had been trying to reach Midwestern settlements but had run into every kind of trouble. As if outlaw bands were not enough, farmers opposed their use of the Shawnee Trail, claiming that longhorns carried tick fever northwards, though they were immune to the disease. And the outlaws were often choice killers who had spent the war in murderous border outfits.

Another hazard, though a peaceful one, were the Indians of the Five Civilised Tribes, who had settled in what is now Oklahoma after being driven from their homes in the Southeast (see Chapter 8). They not unnaturally started demanding toll money from herds passing through their tribal lands. The outlook seemed bleak for cattlemen trying to recover from the war, but at this moment a saviour appeared in the shape of Joseph McCoy, a cattle dealer from Illinois, who was part visionary and part organiser of genius.

The 30-year-old McCoy, realising the urgent need of a trail beyond the settlements, boldly decided to go further and try and swing the cattle trade from St Louis, Missouri, to Chicago. After a long search, he found a tiny township on the railroad that now crossed Kansas, which he decided would make a good shipping point. Its name was Abilene.

It seemed a startling choice. The liveliest spot in a town of a dozen or so long huts was a thriving prairie dog colony in the middle of the main and only street. But McCoy noted the abundance of good grass nearby, and liked the unsettled area around and the fact it was well-watered. Soon he had organised a siding for cattle cars and built pens, and was sending messages south suggesting that Texan drovers might drive their herds to Abilene.

There was already a trail of sorts, blazed by a half-Scots, half-Cherokee trader named Jesse Chisholm, and it was this trail, the immortal Chisolm Trail, that the drovers followed. The first few thousand came up it in 1867 and the boom year, 1871, saw 600,000 longhorns reach Abilene.

Other towns later took over from the first of the cowtowns, wild and woolly spots like Newton, Ellsworth, Hays City, Wichita and the 'Queen of the Cowtowns', Dodge City. All had a season or two of notoriety, and by the '80s, 10 million cattle had passed up the trails to Kansas.

Many cattlemen made fortunes, and beef became the national meat instead of pork. The whole vast migration of cattle spurred on railway development and westward expansion alike, and America was given its most powerful myth, the anonymous American Cowboy, who has been riding the range in the imagination of the world ever since.

This cowboy hostel at Ellsworth in the 1870's had originally been at Abilene but was moved when the latter ceased to be a cowtown. (Kansas State Historical Society).

Front Street, Dodge City, in 1878, showing typical false-fronted township buildings. (Western History Collections, University of Oklahoma Library).

Whether home on the range or going up the trail, the cowboy lived in the saddle. It was beneath his dignity to go on foot unless it was impossible to avoid it. His work was an arduous mixture of boredom, sweat, tension and, sometimes, danger. On the trail, he got used to breathing in clouds of dust, crossing treacherous rivers and enduring extremes of climate. He took stampedes, hostile Indians, outlaws and rustlers not so much in his stride, but as an expected part of his daily life.

He dressed in clothes to suit his work and his face was tanned from the prairie winds and the sun. He was, it has been claimed, the most glamorous hired hand in history, but there was precious little glamour about his hard life. Not that old-timers did not relish their work. 'It sure was a great life,' recalled one, 'and I never knew a cowboy of the old open range that didn't love it.'

Later, the cattle industry became modern, with pedigree cattle replacing longhorns, and with the freedom of the open range giving way to ranches hemmed in with barbed wire. The terrible winter of 1886-87 killed thousands of cattle and a fall in the price of beef helped change the West the old-timers knew. By the turn of the century some cattlemen were even accepting that despised sheep and the even more despised sheepmen had a right to exist in the West. But basically the cowboy's life, in the Southwest and in cattle states like Wyoming, Montana and the Dakotas, went on as before, with the drovers underpaid at about a dollar a day.

Heeker's Cowboys returning to New Mexico from Kansas. Note the Chuck wagon in the background. (Kansas State Historical Society).

The famous Texas Longhorn—descended from cattle brought to America by the Spaniards. The 'T' indicates which ranch the animal belongs to.

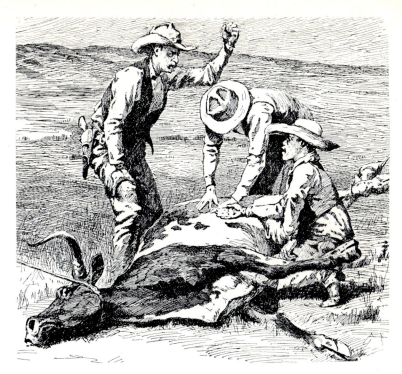

ABOVE: Animals were branded to show ownership and a brand could sometimes be altered by a dishonest rancher and the steer added to his herd. Woe betide him if he was discovered! BELOW: The branding of a steer. Arizona Territory of 1896-99. (National Archives).

The cowboy legend, perpetuated in books, films and on TV, may romanticise an unromantic trade, but is still based on truth. The sudden movement on the trail at night which might start a stampede, if it was not started by a rumble of thunder or some strange group instinct, was the classic moment of danger. Then every cowboy had to force the racing animals into a huge circle. Sometimes a stampede might last for several days. But many nights on the trail were quiet, with cowboys singing to the steers to keep them calm. The tension was always there, though; night guards were always ready to arouse the camp at a moment's notice.

The trails were organised like a military operation. Everyone had a job assigned them. The lookout, usually the trail boss, went ahead, the point riders following at the head of the herd. Other jobs included the wrangler's, who looked after the remuda or extra horses. This usually went to a youngster. 'Cookie' was in charge of the chuck wagon, which was part travelling kitchen, part storeroom—for bedrolls as well as food. Beef, beans, molasses and cornmeal formed the standard menu, which did not give even the most inventive cook much scope. The worst job on the trail belonged to the drag men, bringing up the rear and literally forced to eat dust.

When the cowboy reached town after his trek of more than a thousand miles it was hardly surprising that he often went wild. After a bath and a new suit of clothes—the old ones were filthy and inhabited with vermin —he was ready to enjoy himself in the saloons, at the gambling tables and with the local whores, whose looks varied, as old photographs show, from very passable to frightening.

Until law and order of a sort came to a cowtown, cowboys were liable to shoot up the place for the sheer hell of it. A marshal had to be tough to stand up to these wild Southeners on the spree, and the fact he was likely to have been on the other side in the Civil War did not always

The cowboy's mount—the cow pony—was a tough, half wild animal that ran free until it was four years old and was then rounded up and 'busted'—It's wild spirit was broken, often by a specialist 'bronco buster' who used brutal and speedy methods to tame the animals—he was paid by the head and time meant money. The cowboys used a string of horses and literally wore them out on a drive—he had little time to be kind or sentimental about his mount.

Cowboys select their mounts from the ranch corral.

Muffled against the bitter cold, this cowboy wears fur cap and sheepskin 'chaps' or leggings.

This cowboy, alone on the prairie, awaits gun in hand the approach of strangers— perhaps unfriendly.

LEFT: Joseph McCoy, who turned the tiny hamlet of Abilene into the first great cowtown. (Denver Public Library).

JOSEPH G. McCOY.

help matters. Few cowboys were a match for professional gunslingers, lawmen or otherwise. Their six-guns were often in poor condition and were not, as films would have us believe, always worn in their daily work. So a drunken cowhand loosing off his pistol in a cowtown was a menace to the more sober citizens. But even the most hostile of these had mixed feelings about their unwelcome guests, who brought such prosperity to the cowtowns. Punishments doled out to drovers were on the mild side even by tough lawmen who enforced prohibitions of firearms, fines being the standard penalty. There are no records of a Texas cowboy ever being legally hanged for a killing in the whole gaudy cowtown era.

Most of their bosses were ex-cowboys themselves, but with the difference that they wanted wealth and power, which the average cowboy did not. Some ranchers came from Europe. There were Englishmen, Scotsmen, French and Germans on the range. The reason for the number of Britons, aristocrats among them who mostly had the sense to learn instant democracy, was the amount of British money invested in the West, around $45 million worth by 1880. Most of the ranchers were American, of course, and many had started in other businesses. Richard King, whose descendants run his vast ranch to this day, made his first fortune in steamboats.

In some states, the cattlemen dictated local politics. This was especially so in Wyoming, which became *the* cattle state, and which saw the classic confrontation between cattlemen and settlers, the Johnson County War, dealt with in the next Chapter. To a Wyoming cattleman of 1890 settler meant rustler.

Cattle Kings, like their employees, were no respecters of rank, but of courage and ability. Most of them kept open house to any traveller and a few of them, like John Chisum, were not unlike the average Hollywood rancher. They rarely wore guns. They did not need to, for only a fool with a death wish would try and shoot a rancher down. His cowboys had a lethal way of dealing with assassins which discouraged others. Some ranchers were good bosses, some were not, some worked with their men, others managed their estates from the East or from Britain, putting a local manager in charge.

But the ranchers, even the best of them, remain shadowy figures compared with their hired hands. Why is this? Why is the cowboy the classic figure of the West, far more than the Plains Indian, the cavalryman, the miner or the Mountain Man? Why even today, when cowboys are as handy with jeeps as with horses and sometimes wear sunglasses, does the spell still remain? Is it the epic flavour of the early trailing days, first to the Kansas cowtowns, then as far north as the Canadian border? Even the reality behind the glamorous legend seems to leave the cowboy's supreme position intact.

Perhaps in most people, even the most chairbound, there is the feeling that the open air life is still the best, and that the cowboy and his horse —the one inseparable from the other—are the supreme expression of that life. Few today would really like the prairie for a home, the sky for a roof, but the gut instinct for such a life remains deep in countless millions.

5: Law and Disorder

THE United States was born in violence, and succeeding Frontiers echoed to the sound of gunfire—from time to time. Hollywood has clouded the whole Western scene with gunsmoke, but the real West was at once more violent than any film and more peaceful. It all depended where a man was, and when he was there.

The Wild West is usually taken to mean the trans-Mississippi West, from 1865 to around 1900, but what is 'wild'? The first Wests in Kentucky, Tennessee, and further south and north, during and after the Revolution were infinitely more violent than anything that came later. Indians and settlers savagely fought for possession of the forests, and, even after the Indians had been driven westwards, some of the most ferocious outlaws in modern history, particularly the Harpes, whose trademark was mutilation, made those forests places of terror.

It took a generation to purge the Ohio Valley and the Natchez Trace between Nashville and Natchez of its murderous inhabitants, but the

Dead privates of the 6th Cavalry at Hays City, Kansas, killed in 1873 by a third private of the regiment. (Kansas State Historical Society).

45

climate of violence remained, or travelled westwards. It was the violence of the duel with knife or pistol, of men gouging each other's eyes out or biting off ears. Southerners carried the tradition to the Southwest. Blood feuds kept it simmering, so did Indian wars and the Texas Revolution, but it was the Civil War which saw to it that the trans-Mississippi West should inherit the eastern climate of violence between white and white.

Thousands of ex-soldiers flocked westwards after the war, along with adventurers, gamblers, killers and miners. So, alongside the Settler's and the Cowboy's West grew up another, the Outlaw's West. The three were linked. Not everyone could endure punching cattle for a dollar a day, or farming, when easier pickings were to be made robbing banks, trains and stagecoaches. Most of the notorious badmen of the West, with a few exceptions like the James brothers, were ex-cowhands. So it was that Law—of a sort— had to step in.

It had stepped in earlier, most notably in California, where in Gold Rush days determined men took the law into their own hands to administer prompt, violent justice. The goldfields of 1849 had been cleaned up by miners' courts after criminals had swarmed in along with the honest Forty-Niners, but it was in the booming town of San Fransisco that such instant law reached its notorious perfection.

The city, which, it will be remembered, was only a village before the gold strike of 1848, was a thieves' paradise by 1850. Particularly obnoxious were the Hounds, veterans of the Mexican War, who marched through the streets with bands playing by day and terrorised the citizens, especially Mexicans and South Americans, by night. Public pressure forced them to change their name to the Society of Regulators, but they did not alter their habits. In July, the townspeople rose against them, tried them and—there being no jail—banished them.

Far more serious trouble began in 1851 when ruffians known as the Sydney Ducks (or Coves) turned the city into a jungle after dark. They were mainly British ex-convicts from Australia and their crimes led to the forming of the first vigilance committee, 200 or so leading citizens, who drew up regulations and soon showed the Ducks that they were in earnest. One John Jenkins was caught stealing a safe and was brought before the committee after it had been summoned by the ringing of a bell. Hundreds of ordinary townspeople arrived on the scene and, after a swift trial, Jenkins was hanged from a convenient beam in the street. The police chief was as powerless to act as Jenkins's fellow Ducks.

There were three more hangings, plenty of banishings of undesirables, then, early in 1853, the Vigilantes abolished themselves. They had enjoyed almost universal support. They were back in action again in 1855 to fight against crime as the corrupt city administration would not, but their actions this time were—and remain—more controversial. Yet after hanging several more murderers, they once again disbanded. Even the London *Times* praised their dignified withdrawal from power.

The idea spread. Naturally, some Vigilantes were little better than lynch mobs, but many, in areas totally without law, were not, going about their business like an organised militia, and without masks, like every reputable Vigilante before them.

One of the best efforts by Vigilantes was to rid the West of a veritable Napoleon of crime. This was Henry Plummer, who looked every inch a man of integrity, despite an appalling record of robbery and violence. His final coup was to get himself elected as Sheriff of Bannack, Montana, at a time when he had a 100 strong gang of road agents (highwaymen), whose sole purpose was to relieve miners and other travellers of their possessions. He had lodging houses near the mines staffed by his men, and stage-coaches were marked as being worth robbing. His gang wore special knots in their ties so as to recognise each other and called themselves 'The Innocents'!

The full story of Plummer and his gang, which has been such an inspiration to writers and film-makers, can be read in *The Vigilantes of Montana* a contemporary account by the English editor of the *Montana Post*, Thomas Dimsdale. A few citizens' suspicions were finally aroused, vigilance committees were started, then one of the Innocents confessed. Plummer, drunk with power, did not escape in time and was given one of the most deserved 'necktie parties' in Western history in 1864.

No Vigilantes could have coped with the situation in Kansas and Missouri before the Civil War, where anti-slavery gangs, led by fanatics like John Brown, and equally murderous pro-slavery gangs, killed and destroyed until the outbreak of the war gave them an even greater chance for blood-letting—which they eagerly took. Jesse and Frank James and the Youngers were among those who rode with the barbarous guerilla

Lawrence, Kansas, 1865-1866, was raided during the 'Border War' just before the Civil War. This is a view of it in normal times. (Kansas State Historical Society).

leader, Charles Quantrill, during the war. Jesse was later to become America's Robin Hood, though he did not give cents to the poor and was a ruthless killer. But as a poor, allegedly 'misunderstood', Southern boy who attacked Northern banks, he had plenty of supporters to sing his praises in life and death. Death came in 1882 at the hands of Bob Ford, one of his own gang, who could not resist the lure of the reward put up by railroads which had been more than somewhat troubled by James down the years.

The James Boys lived by their own code, not by a mythical 'Code of the West'. Gunfights at high noon of the sort popularised in films rarely occurred, though Wild Bill Hickok, the 'Prince of Pistoleers' did once have a fight not unlike the sort we so often see. It happened in Springfield, Missouri, in 1865, and he fought one Dave Tutt, with whom he had fallen out over cards and a woman. They faced each other at 75 yards, then, ignoring Hickok's warning, Tutt advanced, drawing his pistol. Wild Bill drew one of his two Colt Navy revolvers, shot Tutt dead, then, so one witness later alleged, asked Tutt's friends, who had drawn, too, 'Aren't you satisfied, gentlemen? Put up your shootin'-irons, or there'll be more dead men here!'

Wild Bill, like so many more, was finally shot from behind, murdered in a Deadwood saloon in 1876 by an unsavoury character named Jack McCall. Even legitimate gunfights were so often messy little affairs at short range, or drunken brawls.

There were few top gunfighters, men like Hickok with nerves of iron, men prepared to kill, who tended to shoot first and worry about questions later. They did their best not to tangle with other leaders in their lethal fraternity. They knew it was dangerous!

ABOVE: Deadwood in 1876. (US Signal Corps, National Archives).
BELOW: Gambling in a saloon at Pecos, Texas in the 1880s. The man seated at table with a white hat is Jim Miller, who was later lynched in Oklahoma in 1909. (Western Historical Collections, University of Oklahoma Library).

ABOVE: *Vigilante justice in Texas, from Frank Leslie's Illustrated News-paper, 1881. (Denver Public Library). BELOW: A saloon fight.*

ABOVE: Gunfighting was less chival-
rous than Hollywood woud have us
believe. BELOW, LEFT: A 'Dude' arrived
from the East is made to dance. RIGHT:
Wild Bill Hickok.

How fast were these old-time gunslingers? Not so fast as modern quick-draw experts with the latest weapons and holsters. Yet how would one of these play-acting gunmen shape up to a Billy the Kid or the cold eyes of John Wesley Hardin, shooting to kill?

Accuracy was the trademark of top gunslingers, lawmen and outlaws alike. Quickness on the draw—from holsters on the hip or the shoulder or from the belt or pocket—was not considered so important as accuracy and taking one's time. Contrary to the myth, many gunfighters had their pistols already drawn. Wyatt Earp had his six-shooter in his hand under his coat as he started to walk with his two brothers and his grisly gun-fighting dentist friend, Doc Holliday, towards Tombstone's OK Corral for their battle with the five-strong Clanton gang. What happened during the minute long gun battle is still hotly disputed, except for the undoubted fact that the Earps won. Earp lived on as a handsome old man until 1929 and was then canonised by a biographer who practically had him win the West. The reaction against him has now reached the point that he is at best regarded as a con man, at worst, as a near-monster. It is Richard III all over again, and somewhere in between the two the real Earp, a minor but interesting Western character, must lie.

As for the 'Code of the West', there was no such thing, unless it was to shoot first and, as we have seen, ask questions later. The law did have certain rules. If you shoot an unarmed man it ranked as murder, but if you shot an armed man, even if he happened to be looking the other way, you would probably be acquitted, even if you were later lynched.

The Law in a cowtown consisted of a marshal, his assistant and several policemen of often variable quality. Abilene began with no law at all. Texans tore the first city jail down and shot up posters suggesting that they should not carry firearms. However, law finally came to Abilene in 1870 in the handsome shape of Marshal Tom Smith, who proceeded to tame the town with sledgehammer fists, weapons that took the Texans by surprise. When Smith, who had been brought up to use his fists on the streets of New York, ordered that firearms were to be parked with saloon store and hotel-keepers, the Texans obeyed. But that November, Smith was murdered, not by cowboys but by two settlers.

The next summer Bill Hickok began his controversial reign with pistols and not his fists. Already afflicted with a reputation, he took pains to survive. As his best biographer, Joseph Rosa, has put it, 'he avoided bright lights and dark alleyways.' His worst moment came when one night he got involved in an argument with the gambler, Phil Coe, who was backed up by around 50 armed Texans. Coe was mortally wounded, but Hickok's deputy and friend, Mike Williams, cut across the line of fire and was killed by a bullet meant for Coe. Stunned by what had happened, Hickok raced through Abilene, clearing every saloon, brothel and gambling den like a man berserk.

Abilene parted with Hickok that fall, and its own days were numbered. Not only did it suggest that cowboys looked elsewhere, but, with the railroad pushing down towards Texas, its status as a cowtown was waning anyway.

ABOVE: John 'Doc' Holliday, gambler, gunfighter, dentist, 1852-87. ABOVE RIGHT: Tom Smith, who literally tamed Abilene with his fists in 1870. RIGHT: Bat Masterton, a gunfighter and lawman who finished up as a New York sports writer. (Kansas State Historical Society).

ABOVE: The Dodge City Peace Commission, left to right Charles Bassett, W. H. Harris, Wyatt Earp, Luke Short, M. F. McClain, Bat Masterson, Neal Brown, 1883. The title of the picture, taken to celebrate Short's return to Dodge after trouble with rivals, was not contemporary. (US Signal Corps, National Archives).

RIGHT: John Wesley Hardin, killer and autobiographer. (Rose Collection, University of Oklahoma Library).

Other towns, like Ellsworth. Wichita and Newton, enjoyed short, violent summers as cattle centres, then faded. Wyatt Earp was never a cowtown marshal, though he was assistant marshal of Dodge for a time. Bat Masterson, who ended his days as a New York sports reporter, served in Dodge, as did Bill Tilghman, who was as near the story book marshal as Hickok was near the gunfighter of legend. Tilghman became one of the greatest Frontier marshals and a living legend in Oklahoma, even liked by some of his enemies. The notorious Bill Doolin once refused to allow his men to assassinate him. 'Bill Tilghman's too good a man to be shot in the back,' he told them. The veteran marshal lasted till he was 70, when a drunken prohibition officer shot him down. He had said he wanted to die with his boots on and he got his wish.

It was one thing to bring law to a cowtown, but in some areas there could be no law except the 'instant' variety. One mining camp in Nevada was 300 miles from the nearest sheriff, and when there was a jail, it was rarely strong enough to stand up to a determined rescue attempt. Only in territorial prisons or state penitentiaries was there some certainty of holding a captive.

Texas was blessed with its famous Rangers whose achievements between 1840-90 almost matched their legend. They were the first to benefit from Samuel Colt's new five-shot revolvers, which made them the scourge of Indians and badmen alike. Later, they were to end the careers of famous figures like Sam Bass (shot) and John Wesley Hardin (imprisoned), and countless smaller fry. Their strength lay in determination, endurance, fine leadership and matchless courage.

Some lesser-known figures had moments of gory glory which no scriptwriter would dare to invent. While a classic cattlemen versus sheepmen war was raging in Pleasant Valley, Arizona, in 1887, Sheriff Commodore Perry Owens, so named after the former naval hero, strode up to a home in Holbrook to arrest a horsethief and found himself taking on a whole family of killers within. In 60 searing seconds he killed three of them, wounded a fourth, and then walked away unscathed.

Range wars and feuds made a mockery of the law. The Lincoln County War in New Mexico lives on partly because of Billy the Kid's part in it. That it was an infamous, bloody conflict, and that Billy was not very similar to the folk hero he has become, cannot disguise the fascination of this miniature civil war and the personalities involved.

One character in the War usually gets less than his due, 'Buckshot Charlie' Roberts. Even the Kid's most violent critics can hardly fail to respond to his daring escape from Lincoln County Courthouse, or become fascinated by the circumstances of his death at the hands of Pat Garrett. And the men whose business interests triggered off the War, John Chisum, the cattle king, John Tunstall, the Englishman whose murder so stirred his employee Billy, Major Murphy and other leading lights all get their popular due. Not so tough old Buckshot Charlie, who found himself surrounded at Blazer's Mill by a posse led by Dick Brewer and the Kid. Before they got him, he had killed Brewer and wounded George Coe and John Middleton, though he was half-crippled before the fight and mortally wounded at the start of it.

ARREST. STAGE ROBBER.

☞ These Circulars are for the use of Officers and Discreet Persons only. ☜

About one o'clock P. M. on the 3d of August, 1877, the down stage between Fort Ross and Russian River, was stopped by a man in disguise, who took from Wells, Fargo & Co.'s express box about $300 in coin and a check for $205 32, on Granger's Bank, San Francisco, in favor of Fisk Bros. On one of the way-bills left with the box, the robber wrote as follows :

> I've labored long and hard for bread—
> For honor and for riches—
> But on my corns too long you've trod,
> You fine haired sons of bitches.
>   BLACK BART, the Poet.

Driver, give my respects to our friend, the other driver; but I really had a notion to hang my old disguise hat on his weather eye.

Respectfully

B. B.

It is believed that he went into the Town of Guernieville about daylight next morning.

———

About three o'clock P. M., July 25th, 1878, the down stage from Quincy, Plumas Co., to Oroville, Butte Co., was stopped by one masked man, and from Wells, Fargo & Co.'s box taken $379 coin, one diamond ring said to be worth $200, and one silver watch valued at $25. In the box, when found next day, was the following   [Fac simile.]

> here I lay me down to sleep
> to wait the coming morrow
> perhaps success perhaps defeat
> And everlasting sorrow
> I've labored long and hard for bread
> for honor and for riches
> But on my corns too long youve trod
> You fine haired sons of Bitches
> let come what will I'll try it on
> My condition can't be worse
> and if theres money in that Box
> Tis munny in my purse
>   Black Bart
>   the Po8

About eight o'clock A. M. of July 30th, 1878, the down stage from La Porte to Oroville was robbed by one man, who took from express box a package of gold specimens valued at $50, silver watch No. 716,996, P. S. Bartlett, maker.

It is certain the first two of these crimes were done by the same man, and there are good reasons to believe that he did the three.

There is a liberal reward offered by the State, and Wells, Fargo & Co. for the arrest and conviction of such offenders. For particulars, see Wells, Fargo & Co.'s "Standing Reward" Posters of July 1st, 1876.

It will be seen from the above that this fellow is a character that would be remembered as a scribbler and something of a wit or wag, and would be likely to leave specimens of his handwriting on hotel registers and other public places.

If arrested, telegraph the undersigned at Sacramento. Any information thankfully received.

J. B. HUME, Special Officer Wells, Fargo & Co.

Poster reproduced courtesy Wells Fargo Bank, History Room, San Francisco.

ABOVE: James B. Hume, Wells Fargo and Co detective who traced Black Bart through a laundry mark on his handkerchief. (Wells Fargo Bank, History Room, San Francisco).

RIGHT: Black Bart (Charles E. Bolton) a famous and very successful stage coach robber with a weakness for verse. (Wells Fargo Bank, History Room, San Francisco).

In such violent times it was hardly surprising that few actual judges made their mark, but a handful managed to, among them the self-appointed Judge Roy Bean, 'the Law west of the Pecos', and 'Hanging Judge' Parker.

Bean was a comic character who dispensed booze with one hand and a sort of justice with the other from his Texas shack known (in honour of the actress, Lily Langtry, whom he adored from afar) as The Jersey Lilly (sic). His most notorious ruling occurred in 1884. A Chinese railroad hand had been slain by an Irishman. Said Bean: 'Gentlemen, the court finds that the law is explicit on the killing of a fellow man, but nothing at all is said about knocking off a Chinaman. Case dismissed!' Drinks were to be on the murderer! Lily Langtry finally reached the spot named for her, when touring the States, but the good judge had died before she ever came near.

Judge Parker ruled in Fort Smith, Arkansas, on the edge of Oklahoma, then Indian Territory, where many tough characters hung out. Business was brisk for his executioner, George Maledon, mass hangings of up to six at a time on a gallows built for twelve, drawing large crowds.

Allan Pinkerton, Founder of the famous firm. (Pinkertons National Detective Agency Inc).

Parker was no Judge Jeffreys, but was a stern Old Testament figure, whose harsh sentences cannot altogether be explained by the exceptionally wild territory he administered. As for the prisoners' cells, they were in the Black Hole of Calcutta class. Juries became reluctant to convict and his final score of actual hangings was a mere 88, done in private after 1891 when Washington stepped in.

When Parker died in 1896 the West was becoming tame, though, as we shall see in the chapter, there was still plenty of life in it yet. Butch Cassidy and the Wild Bunch were still around.

Pinkerton's men led the hunt against Butch as they had against the Renos, who pulled off the world's first train robbery in 1866. Their 'rogues' gallery' of photographs and details of criminals was a key factor in their fight against crime. Jesse James was one of the many outlaws who had reason to hate the Pinkertons, for they probably did more to tame the post-Civil War West than any other body of men. 'I rode 100 miles today', wrote Robert Pinkerton, son of the founder, on one occasion. I am determined that these men must be placed behind bars'. They usually were, or under the ground.

But the Pinkertons had no part in the last classic of the Wild West, the Johnson County War of 1892 in Wyoming. There, the local cattlemen of the Wyoming Stock Growers Association were spectacularly at odds with the homesteaders and squatters on the range. Ever since the Homestead Act of 1862 and other similar laws, settlers had been lured west by the promise of free land, and with them into Wyoming had come rustlers and outlaws. By 1890, ranchers had come to regard homesteaders and rustlers as synonymous.

ABOVE: The classic group photo of the Wild Bunch. Front, left to right: Harry Longbaugh (the Sundance Kid), Ben Kilpatrick, Butch Cassidy. Back, left to right: Bill Carver, Harvey Logan. (Pinkerton's National Detective Agency Inc).

BELOW: The posse who went after the Wild Bunch, and their special train. Chief Special Agent T. T. Kelliher (third from left) was in charge. (Union Pacific Railroad).

Tensions mounted until in exasperation the cattlemen took drastic action. 'Cattle Kate' Watson, who did a brisk trade exchanging her ample charms for cattle, which may or may not have been stolen, was strung up, and so was a storekeeper named Averill who had contested the Association's decision to brand all mavericks—unbranded calves—with its own mark. His store was alleged to be a rustlers' hideout.

The homesteaders of Johnson County elected a Sheriff, Red Angus who was friendly to their cause. Meanwhile, the detectives of the Association drew up a list of 70 rustlers—it is still disputed how many of them were anything else but honest homesteaders who were 'in the way'—then a number of Association members formed a Vigilance committee they called the Regulators.

A score of professional Texan gunfighters were hired, and these killers, plus some local characters, formed an army of 52 which 'invaded' Wyoming in April 1892. The very pro-homesteader historian of the incident, A. S. Mercer, in his classic, *The Banditti of the Plains*, called it 'the crowning infamy of the ages'.

The infamous army was led by a Major Frank Wolcott and a flint-eyed Texan gunfighter called Frank Canton, who was suspected of murdering a respectable settler named John Tisdale the previous November. Newspapermen went along with the expedition which, to those who knew no better, seemed to be a noble body of men destined to put down a reign of terror.

The first target was the K.C. Ranch, belonging to a lion of a man, Nate Champion, whom the cattlemen claimed without any evidence to be a rustler. The invaders had cut all wires in the area to isolate their enemies, but they had reckoned without Champion. With him was a friend, Nick Rae, who was mortally wounded when he stepped out of the hut. Champion dragged him back in, firing at his attackers with his pistol, then fought off his attackers all day and somehow found time to keep a diary of the siege.

Fortunately for Johnson County, a neighbour passed the scene and raced to the homesteaders' town of Buffalo with the news. The attackers finally decided to fire the house by rolling a wagon filled with burning straw down on it. Out came Champion, his six-guns blazing, to die like the hero he was. They stuck a label on him — 'CATTLE THIEVES — BEWARE!' His last entry in his diary had been, 'Shooting again. I think they will fire the house this time. It's not night yet. The house is all fired. Goodbye, boys, if I never see you again. NATHAN D. CHAMPION'.

By now the settlers under Red Angus were roused and the besiegers soon found themselves besieged. The cavalry, sent with the blessing of President Harrison, who was under the impression that Johnson County was in a state of rebellion, rescued the hired army, who sheepishly surrendered their arms to their saviours. Legal battles ensued and the final outcome was that the invaders got off without even a caution. The cattlemen claimed a victory, but the settlers knew who had really won. The homesteaders were there to stay. Cattle rustling, for whatever reason, died down and ranchers and settlers learnt to get along as neighbours.

Guns of the West

by Joseph G. Rosa*

'GOD created man, but it was Sam Colt's revolver that made him equal!' So went the old Frontier saying. Even a physical weakling could stand up to a human gorilla if he knew how to handle a six-shooter.

Guns and the growth of the United States are synonymous. From the early Pennsylvania long rifle—better known as the 'Kentucky'—to the percussion rifles and revolvers of the Civil War, they dominated both the country's battles and its expansion.

But it was the revolver more than any other weapon that helped the plainsman in his trek westwards. Colt's early revolvers were used with devastating effect against the Seminole Indians in the late 1830s, and in the early 1840s by the Texas Rangers to defeat the Comanches. The war with Mexico also saw them in action, but by now they were much improved weapons. They were used in the Crimean War, being the first revolvers purchased by the British Government for issue to troops and sailors. The version issued was the Navy Model of 1851, and some 40,000 of them were actually made in London where Colt had a factory for a short time to make them.

The Civil War finally clinched the fame of Colt's revolvers, and by the time it ended, thousands of them were in the hands of returning troops. There were many rivals to the Colt—the Remington, Whitney, Starr, and Smith and Wesson—but none of them had been produced or used in such numbers.

These early weapons were percussion; that is they had to be loaded with powder and ball, and the charge was set off by a small copper cap filled with fulminate of mercury. This was placed on a small tube or nipple at the back of the chamber and detonated when hit by the hammer.

Colt's revolvers became very popular with cowboys, gunfighters, gamblers and peace officers. Wild Bild Hickok carried a pair of the Navy revolvers, while others, like John Wesley Hardin, preferred the the larger Army weapon.

The successor to the percussion Colt was the 1873 New Model Army, better known as the 'Peacemaker', which became the most famous revolver in the world. Sam Colt never lived to see it, for he had died in 1862, but it was this pistol, more than any other, which immortalised his name.

Originally produced in ·45 calibre with a 7½ inch barrel for Cavalry use, the pistol later appeared in various calibre and barrel lengths. Ammunition for the Peacemaker and its rivals was 'fixed' or metallic. The cap, powder and ball were all contained in a brass or copper case, the method used today.

From 1876, when the Peacemaker became generally available in the West, it was the favourite weapon of many sheriffs, marshals and outlaws together with cowboys, and, apart from a break from 1941-55, it

---

* Author of They Called Him Wild Bill and The Gunfighter.

TOP: Colt's Navy Model of 1851. CENTRE: Colt's Army Model. BOTTOM: Colt 1873 New Army Model, the 'Peacemaker' (Joseph G. Rosa).

BELOW: A Remington rolling block breech loading rifle. In the late 1860s, 27 cowboys armed with this new weapon held off 500 Indian warriors during a cattle drive to Montana. The rifle could fire 17 shots a minute.

has been in production continuously ever since, quite a feat for a weapon which still uses a mechanism designed in 1847!

Equalling the Peacemaker in popular esteem and legend was the Winchester rifle, model of 1873. This ·44-40 calibre weapon (that is a ·44 calibre bullet, propelled by 40 grains of powder) proved so popular that in 1878 the Colt Company rechambered some of their Peacemakers to take its cartridge, and marked each one 'Frontier Six-Shooter'.

Today, the traditions of those sturdy old-timers are carried on by the scores of reproductions, made both for decoration and use, that help perpetuate that part factual, part fictional land, the Old West.

ABOVE: Winchester rifle, Model 1873. (Joseph G. Rosa).

BELOW: Cavalry pistol holster and waistbelt of 1880s, a mixture of Civil War surplus and the revisions suggested in 1874. BOTTOM: The .50 calibre Springfield single shot breech-laying carbine saw a lot of action in the 1870s. Custer's men carried them. They cost $15 to produce and weighed 7½lbs with a range of 600 yards.

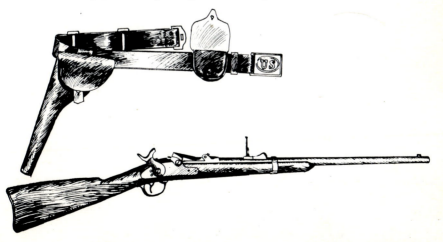

Western costume

MOST Westerners wore the ordinary civilian clothes of their day and usually dressed for the job in hand—in strong clothes for rough work, in suits and hats for business and celebrations. Those who were interested followed fashion as far as their pockets and the availability of garments would let them.

In the early days, when supplies were scarce and white men were few, worn out clothes were replaced by garments made from animal skins, and the comfortable, sensible and hard-wearing clothes of the Indians were often adopted, by some for life. But as the West began to fill, traders shipped out large loads of durable clothes. There were bulk buys from various sources, including homespun suits, sailors' shirts and, after the Civil War, vast quantities of Army surplus, all available to Westerners.

Once permanent settlements were established, the demand came for better clothes and finer materials, and, with increased prosperity, for the very latest fashions. Those engaged in specialised trades found some garments more practical than others. Cowboys took many ideas from their Mexican counterparts, discarded others and, using some of their own, reached a style of dress which—with regional variations—became world-famous. By the end of a trail drive a cowboy's clothes were filthy and verminous, and the first things he liked to do after hitting town were to take a bath, have a shave, get a hair cut and buy new duds.

The lawmen the cowboys met in cowtowns were usually dressed in fashionable gear, which has never appealed to film-makers. As for the uniforms seen in Westerns, they are almost always inaccurate or mythical, unless the film is set in the exact period when Remington was working, and his drawings and paintings are followed closely. Generally speaking, uniforms in films are based vaguely on those in the '90s, even when the films are set in the '50s, '60s, '70s or '80s. The US Cavalry did not wear handsome yellow neckerchiefs, blue shirts and braces for the entire period of the Wild West. They very rarely if ever wore that particular combination at all.

As for the ladies, films, perhaps inevitably, only allow them to look moderately Victorian, with only rarely a suggestion of heavy corsetting. Modern influence creeps into the 'period' clothes of both sexes, but then it always has in the theatre as well. In the 1970s at least, fashions having changed, men can be covered with splendid moustaches and wear their hair longer and therefore more authentically. Apart from one or two short-back-and-sides, clean-cut stars, the 'look' of the Old West on the screen has distinctly improved in one department at least.

BEFORE 1835, the Mexican Army was badly under strength and scattered over a vast area in outposts, it's so-called regiments consisting of a few squads. Some of the officers were veterans of the Spanish Service, and the uniforms, tactics and drill were modelled mainly on out-dated Spanish patterns.

The small Mexican army in Texas had been fighting a spasmodic guerilla war with some of the Anglo-American settlers since 1832, and, when the Revolution broke out, 6,000 raw recruits were quickly raised to combat it. They were hastily armed, equipped and forced marched 1,000 miles across the northern deserts from San Luis Potosi to their rendezvous with immortality at the Alamo.

The march took two months over grim terrain and in weather so bitter that many died of hunger and cold. Many more lived to fight bravely against the legendary defenders of the Alamo.

Mexican Infantryman, 1835

This infantryman is dressed for the great march in blue uniform coat and white canvas trousers. He has tied the chin-straps of his heavy leather shako to his issue canteen, and wears his fatigue, or barrack, cap over a sweat cloth. His musket is a flintlock smoothbore 'Brown Bess'. Many of these muskets were bought by the Mexicans from Britain. The decorative shako cords, overcoats, knapsacks and other encumbrances were removed before the assault on the Alamo.

GAE

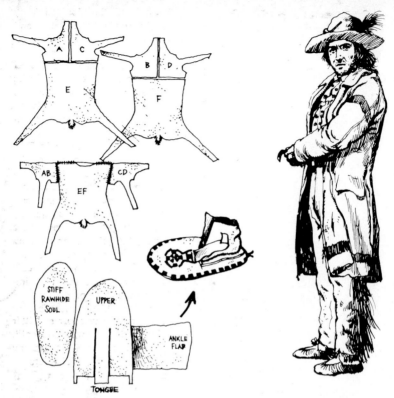

ABOVE, LEFT: Simple deerskin shirt made from two deer skins. Below the pattern is shown a Blackfoot moccasin. These styles of garment were adopted by trappers and mountain men. ABOVE, RIGHT: Early 19th century Rocky Mountain trapper, showing the blanket coat, a long wool and cloth coat popular since the 18th century. Note the fringed trousers and moccasins. BELOW: Men of a survey party in 1870 showing the wide variety of civilian dress worn on the frontier after the Civil War. (Department of the Interior).

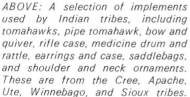

ABOVE: A selection of implements used by Indian tribes, including tomahawks, pipe tomahawk, bow and quiver, rifle case, medicine drum and rattle, earrings and case, saddlebags, and shoulder and neck ornaments. These are from the Cree, Apache, Ute, Winnebago, and Sioux tribes.

ABOVE, RIGHT: Probably taken in the late 1860s, this photo shows Wild Bill Hickok wearing the typical dress of a plainsman and scout. All kinds of fringed shirts and jackets, many decorated with Indian quill and beadwork were worn by Western Dandies. Some Army officers adopted them on campaign not so much because leather was so hard wearing, but because they looked mighty fine. In later years Hickok was something of a Dandy, and like many of hs contemporaries wore the clothes of a typical victorian 'swell'—dark suits, black coat and salt and pepper trousers, white shirts, silk cravats, sashes, gold pins and cuff links, fancy waistcoat and tall silk hats or bowlers.

When the Texas Revolution broke out in 1835, a 'permanent council' passed a resolution to raise 'twenty-five Rangers whose business shall be to range and guard the frontiers between the Brazos and Trinity rivers'. Such was the birth of the Texas Rangers, men who believed, as one of their captains put it, that 'courage is a man who keeps coming on'.

They had no uniforms and they brought their own weapons and horses along with them. Their horses' equipment showed Spanish-Mexican influence, their clothes consisted of rough, strong homespun trousers, thick shirts, fringed buckskins and wide hats.

The first of them carried Plains and Pennysylvania percussion cap rifles, huge knives and a variety of single shot pistols; later, in the early 1840s, they were equipped with early Colt revolvers after the then-struggling Samuel Colt had discussed their needs with Ranger Colonel John C. Hays. They made his name, and Comanches and Mexicans suddenly found themselves facing Rangers who did not dismount to fight them.

To cut his meat, skin animals, chop wood and settle disputes, the early Rangers found their knives handy—Bowies, or Arkansas toothpicks.

Texas Ranger, 1839

This is a typical Ranger outfit of the period. Red was a popular colour for a shirt, while the brown homespun trousers are tucked into boots that were very common at that time. His spurs have rather cruel rowels, the type in fashion during the period that Texas was an independent Republic. Over his shoulder hang a powder horn and bullet bag, and at his waist are his knife and pistol, a US 1836 model, converted from flintlock to percussion.

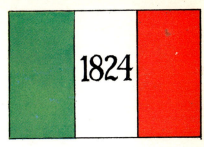

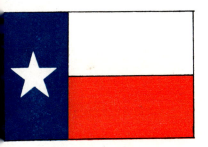

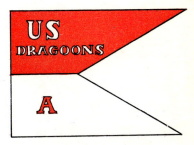

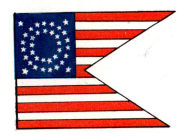

A selection of US Cavalry flags (right) and other flags associated with the American West.

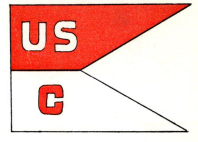

TOP TO BOTTOM: A light coloured Southerner's hat— the 'Planters' hat. A 'wool hat' —the poor man's hat and a term of derision. A commonly worn slouch hat.

Some of the wide variety of rough and workmanlike clothes worn by the Westerner after the Civil War.

On this page two groups of railroad workers are shown. Note the variety of hats and the soft boots of the seated man (above) and (right) the ex-Army greatcoat. *ABOVE, RIGHT: During the Californian Gold Rush of 1849, Levi Strauss, a New York tailor, made hard wearing canvas trousers for the miners. By 1870 these strong blue trousers were worn throughout the West and 'Levis' are now internationally famous.*

The US Army was drastically cut after the War of 1812 ended in 1815, the Cavalry being abolished altogether, apart from a few irregular units. Consequently, when the Frontier moved westwards to the edge of the Plains, infantrymen found themselves ill-equipped to deal with hostile, superbly mobile, mounted Indians.

To combat them, a battalion of Mounted Rangers was raised in 1832 and expanded the following year into the 1st Regiment of US Dragoons, to be followed soon by the 2nd and 3rd. Hard Frontier service and the war against Mexico toughened them into fine soldiers. They took pride in their moustachios—and were the only troops allowed to wear them—on campaign they grew their hair long and wore earrings.

Dragoon, Campaign Dress 1851

This trooper is wearing a dark blue wool jacket, trimmed with yellow worsted braid, and a soft-topped fatigue cap. The caps were sometimes worn with the yellow band shown here, some models having a neck flap that could be let down in bad weather.

The dragoon's waist belt is supported by a narrow white shoulder strap, rather like the British Sam Browne belt. His Hall carbine, a breech-loading single shot percussion smoothbore, hangs from a shoulder sling. To protect his lower legs, he wears 'half-breed' leggings, very common in the West. His neckerchief is a personal addition.

'The Fighting Cheyennes' their greatest historian, George Bird Grinnell, called his most famous book about them. Whether they or the Sioux were 'the finest light cavalry in the world' is a matter for partisans of both great tribes to dispute, but the Cheyennes were without doubt some of the fiercest fighters ever to challenge the American Army in any of its wars.

These proud, handsome Indians had many white admirers among those who fought them. Their battle scars included Sand Creek and the Washita, their battle honours, the Fetterman Fight and the Little Big Horn. As for the fighting retreat of the Northern Cheyennes northwards from an appalling reservation in 1878-79, it is an American epic, one which has inspired historians, novelists and film-makers alike.

The Cheyennes, like the other Plains Indians, rarely had good firearms, and ammunition was scarce. Their primary weapon was a short, powerful war bow, lances, tomahawks and war clubs also being used. They stripped down for battle, ammunition for those who had firearms being carried, along with magic talismans, in small, decorated pouches.

Contrary to popular belief, Plains Indians usually used saddles, and a quirt, or horsewhip, was normally carried from the wrist.

Cheyenne Warrior, 1874

This warrior is painted and stripped for war. His bow and arrows are in a decorated fur case slung across the shoulder in a rather strange but common way. By this time breechclouts were made of bright trade cloth, also used to bind the hair. Note the quirt and the tomahawk.

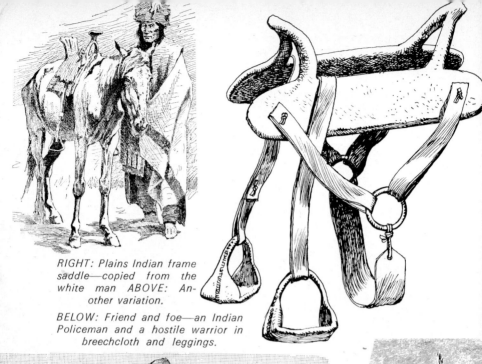

RIGHT: Plains Indian frame saddle—copied from the white man ABOVE: Another variation.

BELOW: Friend and foe—an Indian Policeman and a hostile warrior in breechcloth and leggings.

The cradleboard was used by most tribes for carrying children. It was eminently sensible and often very decorative.

Officers campaigning on the Frontier often wore whatever they felt like wearing, some, like Custer, fighting in buckskins, others in regulation blouses. Most wore navy blue shirts, double- or single-breasted, and sometimes piped with white or yellow. Wives or sweethearts might embroider the collars with crossed sabres and regimental numbers.

Most officers carried rifles, sporting guns or carbines, revolvers, regulation or otherwise, field glasses and map cases. Only officers and NCOs had yellow stripes down the legs of their blue trousers. Regulations permitted the purchase of straw hats for troops serving in hot climates, and this was interpreted very broadly. Major Reno and others wore them at the Little Big Horn. Some officers wore white canvas leggings on occasion.

Officer, US Cavalry, 1880

This officer is wearing a privately purchased light hat and a typical officers' shirt. He has an improvised cartridge belt with the regulation belt buckle, though the Ordnance Department had begun to issue cartridge belts in 1877. Canvas or webbing was preferred because the copper cartridges corroded and stuck in leather ones.

After the Civil War there were large stocks of equipment in hand, and some at least of Custer's 7th Cavalry wore blouses cut down from the old nine button full dress frock coats. The buttons have been found, evenly spaced from neck to waist, on one of the skeletons in the graves of Reno's men excavated some years ago.

Most men wore the regulation five button fatigue blouse of dark blue flannel, and perhaps a few wore the old twelve button short cavalry jacket, trimmed with yellow braid. Dress and equipment varied considerably.

Cartridges were carried in cartridge boxes of different designs, or improvised 'prairie belts'. The men were armed with Springfield Carbines and Colt Peacemakers, both of 1873, at the Little Big Horn, though some officers preferred other weapons. Sabres had been crated and left in store. By the time

the Little Big Horn was reached, uniforms must have been tattered and dust-covered, and equipment showing signs of wear.

Shirts at this date were Army issue grey or, perhaps, navy blue, and in the heat of the day coats were stripped off and carried on the saddles. Hats included broad brimmed greys, floppy black issue campaign hats and even straw hats bought from traders.

Trooper, 7th Cavalry, 1876

This trooper is wearing the five button blouse, black campaign hat and grey shirt described above. He has improvised a canvas and leather belt for his cartridges, and carries his pistol ammunition in an extra short loop attached to its left side. His boots and spurs are regulation issue. Neckerchiefs were not generally worn, and gauntlets were not issued: officers purchased their own.

77

ABOVE: Pre-Civil War United States Cavalry wearing the newly introduced Black felt hat, and Dragoons wearing the low shako of dark blue cloth. Both wear dark blue jackets and sky blue trousers. The cavalry have yellow piping and hat cords, the Dragoons orange. Shown left to right is a red and white cavalry guidon, cavalry trooper, cavalry captain. Dragoon major (mounted). Dragoon and 1st Sergeant of Dragoons in background.

ABOVE: NCO's of the 1st US Infantry during the 1885-86 campaign against the Apaches taken at Turkey Springs, New Mexico. (US National Archives).

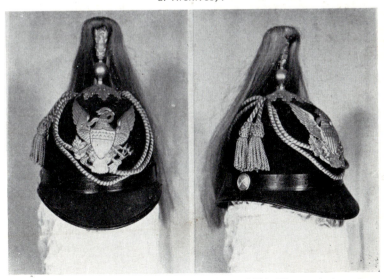

ABOVE: US Cavalry Full Dress helmet, Model 1881. The cords have been wrongly reconstructed. (Marcus Hinton Collection, Photo Michael D. Robson).

Indian scouts serving with the US Army came from several different sources, some belonged to tribes friendly to the Americans, like the Crows and Shoshonis, giving them a better chance to survive against traditional enemies like the Sioux. Others were ex-hostiles like the Cheyennes who, when their wars were over, found military service alongside their old enemies better than idleness on their reservations.

The most famous group of all were the Apache scouts, who were prepared to fight against other Apaches. Without their aid, it would have been virtually impossible for the Army to find some hostile bands, let

GAE

United States Indian Scouts
Corporal, 1890

This scout is wearing the issue uniform, but prefers leggings and moc-casins to Army issue boots. He is examining his new, hooded overcoat, and has already put on his issue canvas gloves.

RIGHT: Sergeant James Frost of the Ute tribe, with guidon. US Scouts (US National Archives). BELOW: Typical Indian Scout.

alone fight them. So strong was the Indians' belief in the independence of the individual that even this extreme form of action was rarely regarded as treachery.

By the late 1880s, scouts were often properly organised and uniformed with both service and full dress, but they usually kept some personal items of equipment and dress. They were issued with grey shirts with especially large collars to take neckerchiefs. Hat cords and NCOs chevrons were white piped red and the cap insignia was white metal, with crossed arrows and the letters USS. For cold weather, scouts were issued with brown skull caps with extensions to protect the ears rather like balaclavas, and with long brown overcoats with pointed hoods. On a scouting mission they sometimes turned their Army blue coats, which were lined with grey material, inside-out for camouflage.

ABOVE: Luther 'Yellowstone' Kelley, a Scout who served against the Nez Perces. (US National Archives). LEFT: William F. Cody—'Buffalo Bill'—the master showman whose early life was exciting enough even when the lies and legends are stripped away. His friends included Wild Bill Hickok, Sitting Bull and the Prince of Wales, later Edward VII. (Kansas State Historical Society).

ABOVE: These two girls were captured by Cheyennes, and returned unharmed in 1875. Women followed fashion closely as they could and often made their clothes themselves. (US National Archives).

Cowboys

Cowboys wore rough clothes for a rough job—A broad brimmed hat to keep off the sun and rain, a large and colourful Bandanna to keep the dust from his nose and mouth, serve as handkerchief, bandage, water filter and towel. Chaps, made of leather (perhaps fur or wool in winter) to protect his legs and boots and spurs. If he carried a gun at all it was kept well out of the way when he was working. Leather chaps ('batwings') and fur chaps ('wodies') are shown below.

Brands

H. Barwise

Flying 7

Stirrup

ABOVE: This trail boss carries full equipment and is prosperous enough to own binoculars. His guns would not normally have been worn when tending cattle. From his saddle hangs his lariat—the rope he used to bring down cattle, hobble horses, drag firewood and, when necessary, hang a thief. (Library of Congress).

Charlie Goodnight

Lazy R

Crazy R

85

ABOVE: The bunk house of a ranch in Clark County, Kansas. BELOW: Who said that cowboys never bathed? They are doing so in either Kansas or Oklahoma. (Kansas State Historical Society). OPPOSITE PAGE: The interior of Sawtell's Ranch, Wyoming Territory, 1872. (Wyoming State Archives and Historical Department).

This Wyoming cowboy has armed himself for the photographer. Note the bandolier of ammunition and the leather covers to the stirrups. (Wyoming State Archive and Historical Department).

6: Trans-
portation
West

THE steamboats reached the West first, before the railroads and stagecoaches. As early as 1818. the first of them laboriously puffed its way up part of the Missouri and, by the 1840s, the Steamboat Age had reached its peak, to decline in the 70s when railways became a more popular form of transport. By then, the steamboats had reached as far north as Forth Benton, Montana. The gold and silver rushes of the previous decade had meant that river traffic boomed in the Northwest.

Some of the steamboats on the Mississippi-Missouri were floating palaces equipped with every luxury that their owner-captains could afford. Others were virtually armour-plated gunboats able to stand up to Indian bullets on the Upper Missouri. All of them looked mighty impressive as their paddles flashed in the sun and thick clouds of smoke belched from their tall funnels.

Journeys could be lively. James Miller, travelling in 1867, noted the remains of a trading post burned down by Indians, and how his own boat rammed another one, 'smashing their cookhouse and seriously disarranging their breakfast.' On the same trip, he rushed on deck and found everyone blazing away at buffalo, then, after dinner one day, saw a 75-strong Indian war party. And that was on a quiet trip! His travels are recorded in *The Road to Virginia City* (University of Oklahoma Press: Editor Andrew Rolle).

Most captains owned their boats and often spent fortunes furnishing them, money they could recover in a season. They were bankers and merchants as well as rivermen. A plantation owner would hand over his crop of cotton or sugar to a captain he trusted, knowing it would be sold at the best market price.

By 1846, there were over 1,000 steamboats on Western rivers, carrying 400 million dollars worth of freight a year. Many were wood-burners and had teams standing by to put out sparks that might ignite the bales of cotton on the decks. Others burnt coal. As a passenger told Charles Dickens, 'They generally blow up forward!' Not surprisingly, the best accommodation was in the rear. The captains coped with everyone from respectable travellers to outright villains, and, before showboats appeared on the rivers, were providing splendid entertainment, as often as not, for their passengers.

The most famous event on the rivers was the race between the *Natchez* and the *Robert E. Lee* from New Orleans to St Louis in 1870, won by the latter; but a far greater epic occurred six years later. The boat was the *Far West*, commanded by Captain Grant Marsh. On June 27, 1876, a Crow Indian came aboard at the mouth of the Little Big Horn River in Montana, to tell him how Custer and his command had been wiped out and the rest of the 7th Cavalry badly mauled. Soon he found himself standing by to rush 52 wounded men 710 miles down the Big Horn, the wild, uncharted Yellowstone and the Missouri to Fort Lincoln.

The nightmare journey through rough waters, with a stop to ferry troops across river and another for supplies, took from the evening of July 3 to 11 pm on July 5, an average of nearly 350 miles a day.

Thanks to Marsh and his men, 51 of the wounded survived. It was a speed record which remained unbroken. Steamboats were still in action in 1898 during the Klondike Stampede, sailing the Yukon and its tributaries, by which time the Stagecoach Age had come and gone.

The first stagecoach king in the West was John Butterfield, who made his fortune in the East, with interests in shipping as well. Then, in 1857, he founded the American Express Company. The next year he gained a sensational contract from the Government, being told to organise a transcontinental stage line. It stretched 2,800 miles from St Louis, into the Southwest through Apache country, then northwards to Los Angeles and San Francisco. Butterfield was a fine organiser, setting up stations every 20 miles, plus wells, and employing 1,800 horses and mules, 250 coaches and 1,000 men. His service ran twice a week, the journey cost 200 dollars, and the trip took 25 days on an average. The first run, from San Francisco to Tipton, Missouri, where it linked up with a railroad, was in 1858.

Within three years, Butterfield's coaches were carrying more mail than were ships sailing between the Atlantic and Pacific. The fabulous Pony Express was to go even faster in its 18 month epic (1860-61), but for all the glamour of its teenage riders, it could not carry enough mail, cheaply enough, and was killed when the transcontinental telegraph began to operate.

A stage coach pulled by four well guarded mules; a more usual form of motive power than the matched horses beloved of the film Western. (US National Archives).

Frank Webner, a Pony Express rider, 1861. Most of the riders were teenagers. (US National Archives).

Butterfield was bought up by an even more remarkable character, Ben Holladay, who sometimes drove his own stages. Stagecoaches were safer than Western films suggest. Even the most daring outlaws could not guarantee to succeed against the 18 people, some heavily armed, who could be crammed aboard a Concord coach, the 'queen of the prairies'. Crammed or not, it was an uncomfortable business. As the *Omaha Herald* advised in 1877, 'Don't imagine for a moment that you are going on a picnic. Expect annoyances, discomfort and some hardship'.

Holladay became known as the Napoleon of the West, but Napoleon suddenly sold out to two brilliant businessmen, Henry Wells and William Fargo, and concentrated on railroads. Wells Fargo soon became the greatest stagecoach network in the West, probably in the world. Today the firm runs armoured car services, audits banks and, in Mexico, is in the travel and hotel business. It is part of the American Express Company, which links it with Butterfield's day. Today, stagecoaches seem as romantic as clipper ships, but travellers then cannot have often thought so. 'Don't grease you hair because travel is dusty,' advised the *Omaha Herald*, which also said that passengers should not growl at the food supplied in stations. Mr Holladay and Co were doing their best!

Henry Wells   William G. Fargo
(Wells Fargo Bank, History Room, San Fransisco)

OPPOSITE PAGE, TOP: 'A Stage Coach Arriving', Painting by Louis Macouillard (Wells Fargo Bank). OPPOSITE PAGE, BOTTOM: 'Perils of the Overland Trail', Painting by H. V. Hansen (Wells Fargo Bank).

RIGHT: General Grenville Dodge, in charge of building the Union Pacific Railway. (Union Pacific Railroad).

In 1862, in the middle of the Civil War, Congress passed an act to build a railroad from the Missouri to Sacramento, California. Eight years earlier, a visionary named Theodore Judah, helping to build small railroads in California, decided it was insane bringing locomotives and rails around Cape Horn, and he began to lobby businessmen and politicians, only to die before work started on the scheme in 1863. Two companies were involved, the Central Pacific from the West, using an army of 10,000, many of them Chinese, and the Union Pacific heading westwards from Omaha, Nebraska, using hordes of Irish and other workers, including many ex-soldiers. These came in handy when Indians attacked, and General Dodge, the engineer in charge, had plenty of natural obstacles to worry about as well.

The backers of the Central Pacific were Leland Stanford, Collis Huntington, Mark Hopkins and Charlie Crocker, who, as we have seen, had made fortunes as merchants in Gold Rush days. Crocker was in charge in the field, and had to cross the Sierra Nevada range, where many of his lightly clad Chinese labourers died. The link-up came at Promontary Point, Utah, on May 10, 1869, where hardheaded Leland Stanford made one of the only mistakes of his life, when he tried to hammer home the golden spike linking the lines on the great day—and missed.

Other railroads were soon to follow, including the Atchison, Topeka and Santa Fe (ATSF), said to 'start from nowhere and go nowhere', though actually it spanned the continent soon after the more northern route. Its bosses had trouble getting to the coast, as Huntington, a typical Robber Baron of the day, demanded vast prices for the right to enter territory he considered his own.

We have seen the importance of the railroad in Kansas to the cattle trade, and now it seemed that the whole continent was being crossed by new lines: by the end of the century there were no less than five transcontinental railroads, as well as the Canadian Pacific, which had been completed in 1885, a key factor in making Canada a united nation from coast to coast. The CPR's railway kings were Scots-Canadians, Donald Smith and George Stephen, and its engineer, an American, William van Horne. They had troubles—rugged terrain, forests, swamps, an uprising of Indians and half breeds, as well as financial worries— and the names of the workers, like their American counterparts, are forgotten if they were ever known, except to cronies. But their influence was colossal. In any state history you are likely to find, say, 'The greatest event in 19th century Arizona was the arrival of the railroad,' not, be it noted, the Gunfight at OK Corral.

The largest group of Union Pacific construction workers ever photographed: Blue Creek, Utah, April, 1869. Many were Irish and most were veterans of the Civil War. (Union Pacific Railroad).

The day that the Union Pacific and Central Pacific met at Promontory, Utah, May 10, 1869. Shaking hands are General Dodge (at right) and Central Pacific's engineer, Samuel Montague. (Union Pacific Railroad).

Settlers at last found it easy to go West, at least to points West on the railroads. After that it was back to the stage, the horse and the wagon. The railroad men put out eye-catching advertisements. In 1888, the Chicago, Kansas and Nebraska Railway—better known as the Rock Island Line—produced a poster tempting people to northern Kansas, 'the finest country in the world', to which you should bring your family and find 'fertile lands, prosperous towns, plenty of churches and schools and NO SALOONS'. Clearly, by 1888, Kansas had 'quietened down some'!

7: Frontier Army

US Cavalry charge into a Cheyenne camp. Painting by Charles Schrey-
vogel. (Library of Congress).

IT needs a major war to stop Anglo-Americans neglecting their armed forces. After the War of 1812, the United States rapidly reduced its Regular Army to 7,500 men, then let it shrink even further. Soon after the Civil War, with its vast numbers on each side, a mere 15,000 men found themselves responsible for the entire Trans-Mississippi West.

The job of this fragment of the victorious Union Army was contradictory. The soldiers protected and opposed the Indians, they seized their land, then had to try and keep interlopers off it. Not surprisingly, the problem was usually beyond the Government whose fighting arm they were, let alone the soldiers themselves. So, like soldiers before and since, they got on with the job, leaving matters of conscience to a few remarkable senior officers, most notably General Crook, whose life was probably shortened trying to help the Apaches he had defeated.

The story of the Indian wars is told all-too-briefly in the next chapter: here the emphasis is on what it was like to serve the Republic, guarding its successive frontiers from the '60s to the '90s.

The pre-Civil War pattern was not so very different, except that in those days of worse communications, forts were even more cut off and boredom, discouragement and lack of promotion led to widespread drunkenness amongst officers and men. Ulysses S. Grant, serving at lonely Fort Humboldt in California, took to the bottle and only escaped court-martial in 1854 because he resigned his commission.

The post-Civil War West was divided into Departments—of Columbia, California, Arizona, Dakota, the Platte, Missouri and Texas. In each were a number of small forts, most of them placed in the middle of nowhere and made of wood or stone. Few post-war forts were surrounded by pallisades after the late '60s because, unbeknown to film-makers, Indians did not attack forts, large or small: they had too much sense. Garrisons ranged from over 200 men to a dozen or so at 'forts' guarding the overland telegraph.

Apart from a few outposts, including Fort Laramie and Fort Riley, Kansas, few ran to two-storied buildings. The average outpost in the wilderness consisted of huts which were stifling in summer and freezing in winter, and which were overcrowded to a degree.

Social life was in short supply, so were women. Before the Civil War, the only woman an enlisted man often saw was an officer's wife, and he had to hope he was stationed near beautiful Cherokee girls, or whatever local talent there was. More women appeared at the posts after the war, and there was always the chance of the occasional dances, beloved by cowboys and soldiers alike. Otherwise, recreations were basically horse-racing, hunting and visits to the overcrowded sutler's store, which served as a club for officers and men.

The food, unless delicacies could be shot locally, was dull, the menus consisting mainly of salt beef, salt pork, dried fruit and vegetables, hardtack, known to sailors as ship's biscuits, or bread if there was a baker on the post, also molasses and strong coffee and stronger whisky.

The men who endured this Spartan life and fought an often elusive, always deadly enemy came from every part of the United States and from Europe. The pre-Civil War Army had mainly been Anglo-

An afternoon of croquet at Fort Bridger, Wyoming in 1873. Officer's quarters are on the left, the hospital and men's barracks are in the right background. (US Signal Corps, National Archives).

American, but immigration brought Germans, Swedes, Swiss and other nationalities into the service and, as always, plenty of Irishmen. There were Scots and Welsh, too, and many born in England. Several Englishmen died with Custer, including Jeremiah Shea from London and James Hathersall of Liverpool. Two other Englishmen, James Pym of Oxford and Jonathan Robert from Surrey, serving under Reno and Benteen, won Congressional Medals of Honour for their bravery on that desperate day in June 1876. And there were ex-Confederates, too, serving with their old enemies in all the Frontier campaigns.

Basic pay for enlisted men was worse than a cowboy's, only 16 dollars a month, which was reduced in the '70s to 13. It was a poor reward for the mixture of danger, boredom and hardwork that the men endured. Promotion for officers was notoriously slow. It might take a Civil War hero, reduced to lieutenant after leading a regiment as a lieutenant-colonel against the Confederates, two decades to make captain.

Though infantry served all over the West, the Cavalry were inevitably the main arm in the post-1865 Indians wars. There were six regiments when the war ended, the Seventh Cavalry being formed in 1866, followed by three more outfits, the Ninth and Tenth being Negro regiments. Cavalrymen often fought on foot, once it was realised that greater fire power could be brought to bear on the enemy in that way. Like the infantry, though, much of their time was spent cutting wood, building roads, etc, and sometimes they escorted wagon trains.

Soldiers used to war in the East needed every help they could get, which meant using civilian guides, including old Jim Bridger himself, and also Indian scouts, mainly from tribes who were the natural enemies of the hostiles. There was no love lost between the Sioux and Cheyenne on one hand and the Shoshonis and Crows on the other. Later, ex-hostiles, including the Northern Cheyennes, who had suffered particularly at white hands, became scouts against the Nez Perce and the Sioux, and the Apache Wars might have gone on for years longer if the hostile Apaches had not been tracked down by their own people. An Indian's independence allowed him to do this early version of doing 'your own thing', and it was better than rotting on a reservation.

'Forty miles a day on beans and hay' was the lot of a good outfit. Its Apache enemies, no respecters of horses, could do 80. The best regimental horses were solid creatures bred in the West, big and strong enough to have a chance of standing up to gruelling marches. Gradually, a minority of officers and men, especially those who served under General Crook, learnt the art of Indian warfare, but always there were recruits to learn the hard way and arrogant officers who

The canteen at Fort Keogh, Montana, in the early 1890's. (US Signal Corps, National Archives).

Camp supply, in Indian Territory, sketched in 1869. It had been built the year before as a base for Sheridan's winter campaign against the and Kiowas. (Western History Collections, University of Oklahoma Library).

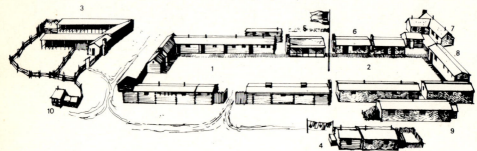

A typical army post of the 1860s and 1870s. There might also be gardens, an ice house, cemetery, and civilian homes outside the fort.

1. Old log fort (pre-Civil War).
2. New extension.
3. Stables and corral.
4. Enlisted men's married quarters ('Suds Row).
5. Commanding officer's quarters.

6. Officers' quarters.
7. Hospital.
8. Quartermaster's stores.
9. Dining hut and kitchen.
10. Sutter.

despised their enemy until it was too late, like the notorious Captain Fetterman, whose story belongs to the next chapter.

Neither Indians nor whites often took prisoners, and most soldiers held a last bullet back for themselves against the very real threat of torture if they were captured. The wounded who were got to safety had to endure fairly primitive treatment in camp hospitals. An arrow wound was regarded as more dangerous than one from a bullet, which might pass straight through the body. Arrows tended to fragment when drawn out. In the long run there was a greater killer than the Indians in the West—disease. The toughest solidiers were no match for TB, pneumonia, typhoid, smallpox and other scourges.

Today, the John Ford film image of the Frontier Army, led at the top by Sherman and Sheridan, by Miles, Crook, Howard, Terry, Custer, Gibbon and the rest, has been tarnished. Ford added to the Remington image romance and a dash of Irish blarney, which was no more untrue than more recent efforts to label the troops as a bunch of brutish killers. Atrocities occurred on both sides, but the most notorious white massacre was perpetrated at Sand Creek in 1864 by 100-day volunteers, not regulars. The truth is that the soldier was far less anti-Indian than the average Westerner, who sincerely believed that the only good Indians were dead ones, a sentiment that goes back much further than Sheridan, who is usually credited with it. Atrocity bred atrocity until Westerners could be found justifying even the slaughter of Indian children on the grounds that 'nits breed lice'.

Meanwhile, the Army got on with its job of fighting scores of 'wars' they were bound to win in the end, often respecting their adversaries in the way that professionals will, and becoming part of the legend of the West, as the Indians so emphatically did.

Sabre exercises at Fort Custer, Montana, 1892. The troopers appear to belong to one of the Negro Regiments. (US Signal Corps, National archives).

SOME FACTS AND FIGURES

From 1865 to 1898 the Regular Army fought 938 engagements with the Indians, including 'battles' which were mere skirmishes.

* * * * *

59 officers and 860 enlisted men were killed in this period.

* * * * *

In 1869, the Army consisted of 25 regiments of infantry, 10 of cavalry and five of artillery. In the mid-70s, when the Indian wars were still raging in many parts of the West, the entire Army was a mere 25,000 men, a figure that remained static until the Spanish-American War of 1898 broke out.

* * * * *

The Cavalry used Springfield carbines and Colt's revolver. Sabres were issued, but were usually left behind on Indian campaigns.

* * * * *

Springfields were the Army issue rifles and carbines from 1873-92, but a wide variety of others were used as well, notably Sharp's and Remington's breech-loading repeating weapons.

* * * * *

Artillery was not much used in the Indian wars. Gatling guns do not seem to have been very effective, but rapid-fire Hotchkiss guns were more successful in campaigns which included the Nez Perce War and Wounded Knee. The Modoc War of 1872-73 was a rare occasion when howitzers and mortars were used to try—without success—to blast the Indians out of their stronghold.

* * * * *

ABOVE: *Hard bitten officers and troopers of the US Cavalry in the 1870's show the wear and tear of hard campaigning. (US National Archives).*

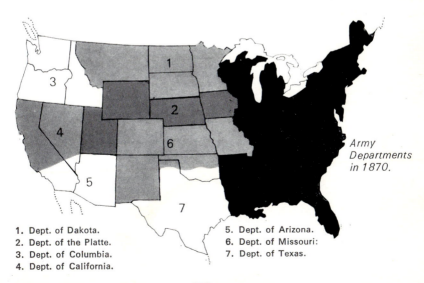

Army Departments in 1870.

1. Dept. of Dakota.
2. Dept. of the Platte.
3. Dept. of Columbia.
4. Dept. of California.

5. Dept. of Arizona.
6. Dept. of Missouri:
7. Dept. of Texas.

8: The Indians' Last Stands

IN the winning of the West the Indians were always the losers, even in their moments of victory. The last faint chance of driving the white men into the sea had been Pontiac's Rebellion of 1763, which foundered because of the traditional impossibility of keeping different tribes united against a common enemy. Indian democracy often resembled anarchy in time of war and, contrary to legend, chiefs rarely had power in the white's sense.

From the 1770s, when the first settlers crossing the Appalachians, the Indians were always candidates for removal further west or for extinction, valiantly as so many of them fought. First Joseph Brant, the great Mohawk, during and after the Revolutionary War, then Tecumseh, the Shawnee before and during the War of 1812 tried to unite the tribes against the Americans. But Indians lost the old Northwest in the 1790s, the settlers pushed steadily westwards, and by the 1830s, the Plains Indians, though they did not know it, were threatened.

When Columbus reached the New World there had been perhaps a million Indians in what became the United States, Stone Age warriors and farmers without the horse. To talk of Indians is as dangerous a generalisation as to talk of Asians or Africans, yet Indians had certain things in common. They worshipped the Sun and the Earth. They did not own the Earth. How could one own one's mother? This did not prevent them disputing hunting rights in certain areas, or spheres of influence; besides, most of them were warriors.

But it was not all war. Red Indians enjoyed—and still enjoy—rich family lives and their children were adored to the point of indulgence. But in war an Indian's aim was often terror. Torture, which some tribes developed to almost as fine an art as their 'civilised' European contemporaries, sometimes had religous overtones and was a form of release as well as revenge. The Iroquois especially honoured their victims (when they were not adopting them) and the victim himself was more honoured if he sang his defiance at his captors.

Across the Mississippi less advanced tribes than the mighty Iroquois lived slow lives, hunting the buffalo, which gave them food, shelter and clothing, on foot. Dogs dragged their belongings. But by the mid-18th century, the Plains Indians had become horsemen, incomparable horsemen, and this revolution started them on a Homeric way of life which still thrills so many nearly a century after it finally ended in slaughter and bitter defeat.

The buffalo hunt became a thing of splendour and excitement; war was more exciting than ever when waged on horseback; and horse-stealing became the greatest game of all. Even worthier than killing an enemy was counting coup on him—touching him. Down in the Southwest the Apaches were not so concerned with Indian chivalry. Their story follows later.

An Indian 'travois'—a framework of poles dragged by a pony which was used to transport their lodge poles and buffalo skin lodges, etc.

In the age of the Mountain Men, the Plains Indian, with no one wanting his land, and with no gold found as yet in California, seemed a creature of Romance, the noble savage of legend as opposed to the 'painted fiend' he was to be dubbed when he was found to be 'in the way'. Yet it was in this period, the 1820s and '30s, that the Five Civilised Tribes of the Southeast, the Cherokees, Creeks, Choctaws, Chickasaws and Seminoles, the most advanced Indians on the Continent, were forced to abandon their homes and to settle in Indian Territory, now Oklahoma. Their doom was finally settled when Andrew Jackson became President in 1828, a man whose attitude to Indians was strictly Frontier, and who was dedicated to remove not only hostile tribes from the South, but tribes which had actually fought for him.

The most infamous of several 'trails of tears' was the Cherokees' in 1838-39 on which 4,000 out of 13,000 perished. Thanks to Sequoyah, the inventor of their alphabet, these same Cherokees were literate almost to a man. Their standard of living in the South had become higher than the average white man's. Even the Supreme Court thundered against the State of Georgia's wrongs against them, but Jackson overruled it. Only a handful escaped into the wilds and their descendants now live in North Carolina.

A rare photograph of the 'Sun Dance' a deeply significant ceremony during which a warrior proved himself. Skewers were thrust through the warrior's flesh and ropes attached to them by which he hung until the skewers broke free.

Some of the Seminoles went west, but others fought in the swamps of Florida with such desperate courage that, after three wars which cost the USA $20 million and 1,500 men, some of the surviving Indians remained unconquered. Their descendants, too, survive as reminders of their ancestors' valour in nightmarish campaigns.

Soon it was the time for the Plains Indians, the Sioux, Cheyennes, Blackfeet and the rest to find that there was no stemming the white tide. The first great uprising happened in Minnesota, while the Civil War was raging and troops in the forts were few. The Minnesota Sioux had plenty of genuine grievances: land encroachments, shortage of promised food, unscrupulous traders. One of them, Andrew Myrick, sneered: 'If they're hungry, let them eat grass!' When the outbreak occurred in the summer of 1862, led by Little Crow, it was a terrible one. Myrick got his deserts, the mouth of his dead body stuffed with grass, but 700 settlers and 100 soldiers died before it was over. Some chiefs were hanged, and the Minnesota Sioux were driven westwards, except for some who were given sanctuary in Canada.

For 30 years after the uprising there was rarely peace on the Plains. By far the worst of the punitive expeditions—whose normal result was to inflame the Indians still further—was the massacre perpetrated by the Reverend J. M. Chivington and his Colorado volunteers, who, in 1864, butchered Black Kettle's band of Cheyennes at Sand Creek, killing perhaps 200 women and children and 70 mainly unarmed men, also 40 or so Arapahoes. Figures have been disputed, apologists have stressed previous Indian atrocities and the fact that young warriors may have been away on the warpath from the camp, however peaceful it seemed. Not in dispute is the fact that Black Kettle longed for peace, that he was at Sand Creek on military advice, that, when the attack started, the American and a white flag were run up over the Chief's tent, and that, as he stood singing his death song, he chanted 'Nothing lives long, except the earth and the mountains'.

The volunteers carried scalps back to Denver along with severed limbs, to be greeted with cheers. But most Americans, even hardened Westerners, were sickened. Kit Carson, who had killed his share of Indians in his time, called Chivington and his men cowards and dogs. The only result of the massacre was worse Indian trouble.

The story of the years that followed is too rich in incident to be more than sketched here. Among its highlights was Red Cloud's War. In 1865, it was decided to protect the Bozeman Trail, running from Fort Laramie, Wyoming, to the goldfields of Montana, with a military road and a series of forts. Red Cloud, the great Oglala Sioux leader, refused to sign a treaty for the road, rightly claiming that it violated earlier ones.

Colonel Henry Carrington was given the job of building the forts the most famous of which, Fort Phil Kearny, was his beleaguered headquarters. In December 1866, a classic Indian victory occurred near the fort, when an arrogant hothead, Captain William Fetterman, having several times boasted, 'Give me 80 men and I'll ride through the whole Sioux Nation', got his chance from a reluctant Carrington. He rode out with a command of 81 men, was lured beyond the safety limit, and was attacked by Sioux, Cheyennes and Arapahoes. Among the Indians who wiped out the entire force was a young Oglala Sioux, Crazy Horse, destined for immortality.

Though the Americans got their revenge at the Wagon-box fight, when their new breech-loading rifle mauled their attackers, this was a war the Indians won. In 1868, the troops were ordered out of the Powder River country and also the Black Hills 'for ever'. Red Cloud had the supreme satisfaction of seeing his warriors burn Fort Phil Kearny to the ground.

Having signed a treaty, he never went on the warpath again, though he pleaded the cause of the Indian in Washington and elsewhere to enthralled but impotent audiences. But the younger warriors were ready to continue fighting.

The situation by the '70s was becoming even more desperate for the Indians, with the gigantic buffalo herds almost exterminated, the railroads transforming the West, and settlers hurrying to live on

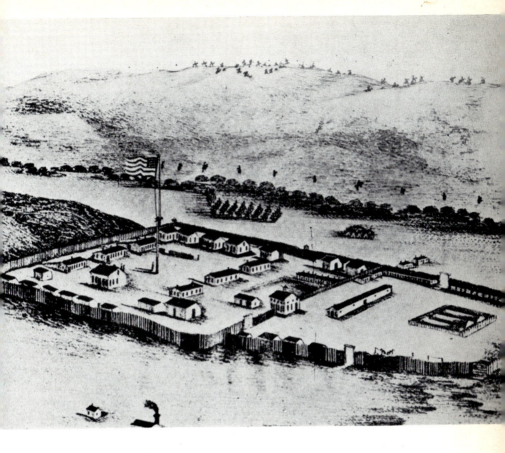

ABOVE: Fort Phil Kearny in 1886. (Wyoming States Archives and Historical Department).

RIGHT: Colonel Carrington, in command of Fort Phil Kearny in 1866, and held responsible for Fetterman's folly. (US Signal Corps, National Archives) OVERLEAF: The Fetterman massacre of Sioux and Cheyennes followed a series of boasts by Captain Fetterman. 'Give me 80 men and I'll ride through the whole Sioux nation', was the standard one. TOP LEFT: Fetterman. TOP RIGHT: Captain Ten Eyck who went to his relief. BELOW: A map of the fight on December 21, 1866. (US Signal Corps, National Archives).

Fetterman, who led the troops in the disastrous fight of December 21, 1866

Captain Ten Eyck, who was sent to th Captain Fetterman

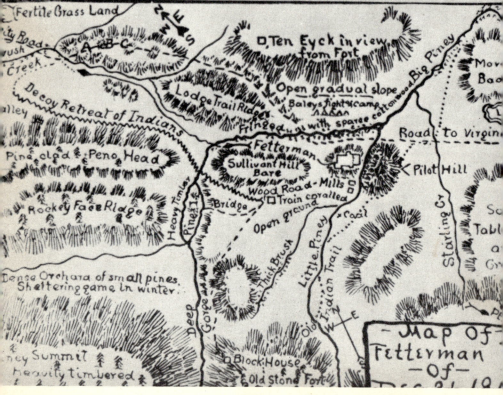

Fertile Grass Land

Ten Eyck in view from Fort

Road

Brush

Creek

A B C

Decoy Retreat of Indians

Lodge Trail Ridge

Open gradual slope

Baleys fight camp

Fringed with sparce cottonwood

Big Piney

Mov Bad

Road to Virgin

Valley

Pine clad Peno Head

Fetterman

Sullivant Hill Bare

Wood Road Mills

Train corralled

Pilot Hill

Rockey Face Ridge

Bridge

Open ground

Cecil

Heavy Timber

Pinery

Little Piney

Starling Cr

So Tabl a Gr

Dense Orchard of small pines. Sheltering game in winter.

Thick Brush

Old Indian Trail

Deep Gorge

Block House

Old Stone Fort

Map Of Fetterman -Of-

ney Summit heavily timbered

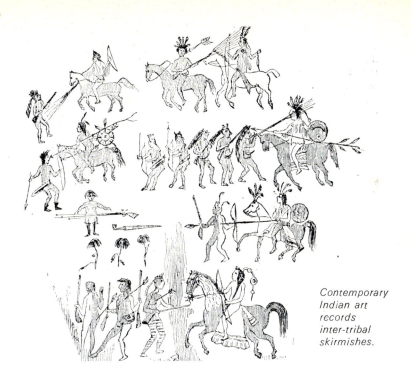

Contemporary
Indian art
records
inter-tribal
skirmishes.

what had once been regarded as the Great American Desert. The discovery of gold in the Black Hills of Dakota in 1874 led directly to the Battle of the Little Big Horn in Montana on June 25, 1876. Custer's Last Stand was virtually to be the last stand of the Plains Indians as well, but it was a stirring moment when the glory-hunting Custer and his 200 men blundered into a huge gathering of Sioux, Cheyennes and some Arapahoes after fatally dividing his Seventh Cavalry into four detachments. After a bitter fight of an hour or so, several thousand Indians under Crazy Horse, Gall, Sitting Bull, Two Moon and other war chiefs had not only wiped out Custer's entire command but badly mauled the rest of the regiment. The 'facts' have been disputed ever since, for the Indians were reluctant to talk for many years and, besides, there was a pall of gunsmoke over the battlefield.

George Armstrong Custer, 1839-76, as a Major General in 1865. (US Signal Corps, National Archives).

ABOVE: Captain Frederick W. Benteen, who gradually assumed command though not in name, at the Little Big Horn after Custer and his men disappeared. (National Park Service, Department of the Interior).

ABOVE: Gall, a war chief of the Sioux at the Little Big Horn, and one of the leaders in the fight. (National Park Service, Department of the Interior).

BELOW: Grave of the 7th Cavalry, Custer's Command. (US National Archives).

Major Marcus A. Reno, in full dress uniform, made the scapegoat of the Custer fight. The original plate has suffered an accident causing a white 'blob' to appear. (National Park Service, Department of the Interior).

The Plains never saw an Indian gathering like that again and, by the following year, most of the hostiles had been defeated, rounded up, or, in the case of Sitting Bull and several thousand fugitives, had fled to Canada. Because food was in short supply for Canada's Indians, the handful of North-West Mounted Police who found themselves in charge of Sioux warriors with the scalps of Custer's men at their belts, had to try and get them to return, though the Sioux had hoped to settle. There was always the danger of trouble between the American

ABOVE: Officer's of Crook's command pose with the 7th Cavalry Guidon for a photograph in the captured Sioux camp. Booty from the little Big Horn was found among the lodges. (US National Archives).

ABOVE: Sitting Bull, the most famous and distinguished of all the Sioux. A medicine man and warrior, he was killed by Indian police in 1890. (Smithsonian Institution, National Anthropological Archives).

and Canadian warrior tribes, which made the Mounties calm control of the situation a notable chapter in Canadian history. Finally, the last of the Sioux, with Sitting Bull, returned to American soil in 1881.

Less than a decade later the great Sitting Bull was shot dead by Indian police shortly before the final confrontation of the Indian wars, the massacre at Wounded Knee in January 1890, which the whites called a battle.

Muleskinners load a mule for General Crook's Yellowstone expedition.
(US National Archives).

ABOVE: US Cavalry Captain's full dress epaulettes. According to the
1882 Regulations the regimental number should be in the centre of
the yellow pad, between the pairs of silver captain's bars. (Marcus
Hinton Collection, Photo: Michael D. Robson).

ABOVE: Dull Knife of the Northern Cheyennes speaking to his captors at Fort Robinson, Nebraska, before the Indian's heroic breakout and last stand. (Nebraska State Historical Society).

Between the Little Big Horn and Wounded Knee there were a number of Indian last stands, some famous, some forgotten, some immortal. The Northern Cheyennes were sent to Indian Territory in 1877, where the Southern Cheyennes had been moved earlier, but the climate and desert-like conditions proved too much for them. In despair they headed north towards their old home in 1878, led by Dull Knife and Little Wolf, and pursued by troops across land now thick with settlements and criss-crossed by railroads.

ABOVE: Fort Robinson, Nebraska, in 1883. The earlier barracks from which Dull Knife's band broke out was similar to this. (Nebraska State Historical Society).

A division of opinion caused a split, which led to Little Wolf, the warrior, taking part of the Cheyennes to Montana, where they were finally allowed to remain. The rest under old Dull Knife, who believed that the Americans would allow them to stay in the north, were captured and taken to Fort Robinson, Nebraska. Too late, they realised their mistake and broke out, men, women and children, starving, dressed in rags and pitifully armed, to die in snow made red with Indian blood because they could not bear to be returned to their desert reservation.

ABOVE: Young Man Afraid of His Horses, a Sioux chief whose name really meant that he was so great a warrior that even his horses inspired fear. (Nebraska State Historical Society).

ABOVE: Little Big Man, Sioux Warrior. When a peace commission was sent to try and persuade the Sioux to part with their beloved Black Hills, Little Big Man wanted war.

Lowdog, A Sioux chief who played his part in the defeat of Custer.

Far to the West in northern California a little-known tribe called the Modocs also made a striking last stand. We have seen in the Gold Rush chapter how California's Indians, were almost exterminated, but the Modocs, unlike many Far Western Indians were warriors and born fighters. Injustice caused a band of about 50 of them, led by Captain Jack, to attack settlers, then retreat to almost impregnable natural fortifications, the Lava Beds near Tule Lake, in January 1873. They lasted out until May, inflicting humiliatingly heavy casualities on the Americans, and would have lasted longer if it had not been for fatal divisions in the Modoc camp, and the equally fatal murder of General Canby, a sincere friend of Indians, under a flag of truce, which had the nation howling for their blood. Five Indians were killed in

Captain Jack, leader of the Modocs in their fight against the Army, 1872-73. He was later hanged. (Smithsonian Institution, National Anthropological Archives).

the war and 82 soldiers and civilians. Before Captain Jack was hanged he tried to defend himself: 'I have always tried to live peaceably and never asked any man for anything . . .', but it did him no good.

A greater man and greater orator, who at least escaped hanging, was Chief Joseph of the Nez Perces. Even the least sentimental could hardly deny that he was one of the noblest of all Americans.

Joseph's people lived in beautiful country in Oregon and Idaho. Their name had been given them by 18th century French trappers because they had sometimes worn nose ornaments. They were as handsome as any Indian on the continent, intelligent, advanced, and were cleaner than most Indians and many white men. They had never killed a white man and were highly regarded, except by hard line Indian haters.

In 1877, the Government, urged by settlers, tried to move Joseph's Lower Nez Perces from their lovely Wallowa Valley. It was the old story. Joseph refused and there was a minor Indian outbreak, which did not have his sanction; but, with war inevitable, he took command of 250 warriors and many more women and children, and began an epic fighting retreat.

He defeated the first troops sent against him, then, joined by a noted warrior, Looking Glass, and his band, headed for a new life on the Plains. But it soon became obvious that their only hope was to reach Canada and British protection. In battles and skirmishes, they defeated their pursuers, and from beginning to end of their march not a settler was harmed. Slowed down by women and children, the Indians marched 2,000 miles, with 5,000 troops after them, but finally, in Montana, only 30 miles from Canada and safety, and after a ferocious battle in a snowstorm, Joseph surrendered. To his victor, General Miles, he then made the grandest, saddest speech in Indian history, part of which went—'I am tired of fighting . . . It is cold and we have no blankets. The little children are freezing to death . . . Hear me, my chiefs. I am tired; my heart is sick and sad. From where the Sun now stands, I will fight no more forever.'

Despite promises by Miles, who remained his friend for life, that the Nez Perces would be sent home, they were condemned to rot in Indian Territory, where many of them died. After pressure from white

Typical Indian dress of the late 1800s with the man wearing ex-Army trousers, and the squaw, a calico dress obtained from an Indian trader.

sympathisers, the survivors were sent back to the Northwest, but not to their homes. Joseph visited Washington as an honoured guest, but he died in 1904 on a reservation far from his beloved valley, which he never saw again.

In the Southwest, the Comanches, were finally subdued in 1874. Matchless horsemen, even by Indian standards, they had caused havoc in Texas for so long that they were given a reservation outside the state in Indian Territory. Their greatest chief, Quanah Parker, the half-white son of Cynthia Ann Parker, who had pined away when she was returned to her own people after years with the Comanches as a captive and a wife, became as notable and colourful figure in peace as he had been in war.

But the Apaches were still unsubdued. Nowadays over-glamorised as freedom fighters by the ignorant, who do not know how they were hated by most other tribes in the Southwest on whom they had preyed for centuries, they yet were heroic figures who deserve their fame.

The US Government, aided by corruption and incompetence on a vast scale, asked for the Apache Wars and got them with a vengeance which can chill the blood a century later. These tigers of the desert did not regard war as a great game. They could live off the desert like lizards, run 40 miles a day and ride 80 or more. Their tactics were ambush, torture and sudden death, carried out down the centuries with dedicated ruthlessness. Not for Apache boys the idyllic childhood of so many Indian children. They were trained to run for miles with water in their mouth and not swallow it, not just as a discipline but to make them breath properly. They also ran with loads on their backs, as well as learning to handle weapons from infancy.

Racial hatred between the Mexicans and Apaches was traditional by the mid-19th century, the former using bounty hunters, treachery and mass murder to try and exterminate the Apaches, the survivors repaying them with massacres and often diabolical tortures. There were probably never more than 4 to 6,000 Apaches, actually several linguistically related tribes, who rarely fought as one. They were related to the Navahos and their name was—suitably—a Zuni Indian word for enemy.

In 1853, the Gadsden Purchase from Mexico—an extension of Arizona and New Mexico—gave the very heart of Apacheria to the

Naiche, son of Cochise, and his wife.

127

Lieutenant George Bascom, whose inexperience and prejudice helped provoke the greatest of the Apache wars. He was later killed in the Civil War. (US Signal Corps, National Archives).

USA. The Apaches had hoped to be friendly with the Americans, but it proved impossible, one reason being the brutal flogging of the remarkable Mangas Coloradas by white miners in New Mexico, who objected to the old warrior watching them at work.

His son-in-law, Cochise of the Chiricahuas, deciding that the only hope of survival for his tribe was to keep peace with the Americans, held back from fighting them until 1861, when he was wrongly accused by George Bascom, a callow young lieutenant straight from West Point, of kidnapping a white boy, who was actually half Indian. Cochise, whose men cut wood for a stagecoach station in Apache Pass, had come willingly to Bascom's tent. According to the usual version of what happened next, he left, slashing his way out, with a bullet tearing into his leg. Six Apaches were seized as hostages, and Cochise took white prisoners. The execution of first the Indians, then the whites triggered off a 26 year nightmare for which Bascom is usually blamed. Probably war was inevitable, and it seems that it was the arrival of a superior, Army Sugeon Irwin, which precipitated the order to hang the Apaches, with the result that Cochise soon joined Mangas Coloradas in total, pitiless war.

Cochise made peace in 1872, nine years after Mangas had been captured by a ruse, then killed 'attempting to escape'. During those years Cochise made the Chiricahuas a byword for cruelty at a time when it was official policy to exterminate them. Except when first faced with artillery, the Indians were invincible. In 1871, the extermination policy was reversed after a particularly unsavoury massacre of peaceful Apaches, but Cochise only made peace because of the trust he had in a tall, bearded frontiersman, Tom Jeffords, who led the deeply religious General Oliver O. Howard to his stronghold to parley with him.

Jeffords, at a time when it seemed that no white saw Cochise and lived had struck up a friendship with Cochise after daring to visit him. He was in charge of the mail between Tucson and Fort Bowie and, finding that his men were little more than a suicide squad, rode into

This is an exciting game played by Apache youngsters, in the early eighties, at San Carlos, Arizona.

ABOVE: This picture gives a good impression of the notorious San Carlos Reservation, where most Apaches were herded in the 1870s. (Western History Collections, University of Oklahoma Library). BELOW: General O. O. Howard, a one-armed Civil War veteran who made peace with Cochise in 1872 and fought Chief Joseph in 1877. (US National Archives).

the stronghold and asked that his harmless mailmen be allowed through. The two extraordinary men became blood brothers, and when Howard and Cochise made peace, Jeffords became the Chiricahuas' agent, their reservation being their beloved Chiricahua Mountains.

Cochise died in 1874 and with brutish lack of decency and sense, the Chiricahaus were sent two years later to the appalling San Carlos reservation where other tribes were herded to rot in unhealthy conditions. Jeffords resigned in disgust.

ABOVE: General Crook with his scouts Dutchy (left) and Alchise, also his mule, Apache. A humane man, who was also the finest Indian fighting general. (US Signal Corps, National Archives)

OPPOSITE PAGE: Geronimo, the most famous, though not the greatest, of the Apaches. This suitably posed picture was taken in 1886, the year of his final surrender. (Smithsonian Institution, National Anthropological Archives).

There followed ten bitter years of mismanagement, and outbreaks from the reservation by small bands led by legendary fighters like Victorio and old Nana, who, after the former's death, led a band of around 15, then 40, Indians for two months. He fought off hundreds of troops on both sides of the border, along with Texas Rangers, civilians and Mexicans. At the time Nana was probably 80!

The Army was hopelessly handicapped by graft and corruption in official circles, yet General Crook and a band of devoted young officers, sensibly using Apache scouts, learnt how to fight the Apaches. Crook, a man of integrity once insisted: 'I have never yet seen (an Indian) so demoralised that he was not an example in honour and nobility compared to the wretches who plunder him of the little our government appropriates for him'.

ABOVE: General Nelson A. Miles, photographed in 1900, when he was chief of the US Army. A notable Indian-fighter, he was extremly ambitious and courted publicity. (Arizona Historical Society).

The last outbreaks were dominated by the much-publicised Geronimo. Crook, sent north to fight the Sioux in 1875, was hurried back in 1882 to take control. In 1886, he seemed to have finally ended Geronimo's spectacular career, but an obscene drink-peddlar inflamed the apparently resigned Apaches and, on March 28, 1886, Geronimo, Nachez (or Naiche), Cochise's son, together with 20 warriors, 13 women and 6 children, fled for the wilds of the Sierra Madre. The bootlegger, one Tribolett, may have been put up to the job by those who were making a fortune from the war.

Crook promptly resigned after Sheridan had questioned the loyalty of his scouts and his methods, and was replaced by the ambitious cold but skilled General Nelson A. Miles. He finished off the Apache Wars by means of a picked flying column, and by using heliographs and a few Apache Scouts. Meanwhile, he treacherously rounded up many peaceful Apaches and sent them to a Florida prison camp and—final infamy—dispatched Crook's loyal scouts along as well to share the exile of Geronimo and his band, who finally surrendered in September 1886.

ABOVE: This famous photograph shows Geronimo and his band resting beside the Southern Pacific Railroad near Nueces River, Texas, on September 10, 1886. The Apache Wars were finally over and the last hostiles were on their way to a prison camp in Florida. Geronimo is in the front row, third from the right. Some wives can be seen in the background. (US National Archives).

Only the efforts of Crook and other wellwishers got the surviving Apaches out of Florida, whose climate was death to them. Crook visited them in Alabama in 1890 just before he died of a heart attack; later the Apaches were moved to Indian Territory and finally, in 1907, those who wished to were allowed to live with the Mescaleros in New Mexico. In 1909, Geronimo died at Fort Sill, having earlier enjoyed riding in Theodore Roosevelt's Inaugral Procession.

So peace came to the blazing Southwest, though, typically, one Apache, Massai, caused the Army much trouble after leaping from his prison train en route for Florida, returning 1,000 miles undetected, and waging a one-man-war for a time before vanishing from history and into legend. It is hardly surprising that today Apaches make better cowboys than farmers. Blood will tell.

*F. W. Loring of Boston, correspondent for Appleton's Journal went with
Lieutenant Wheeler's survey expedition and this photograph was taken
four hours before he was killed by Apaches on November 5, 1871. (US
National Archives).*

The frozen body of Big Foot, whose band was almost exterminated at Wounded Knee in December 1890. (Smithsonian Institution, National Anthropological Archives).

There were a few minor outbreaks in the West after the Indian Wars officially closed at Wounded Knee in 1890, but they meant nothing, except to the despairing men who suddenly turned to useless action. Charles Russell, artist, cowboy and Indian-lover at a time when it was unfashionable, put the whole sad, glorious story into few simple words:

'The Red man was the true American. They have almost all gone, but will never be forgotten. The history of how they fought for their country is written in blood, a stain that time cannot grind out. Their God was the sun their church all out doors. Their only book was nature and they knew all the pages'.

ABOVE: Officers of the 6th US Cavalry Regiment, some of whom fought at Wounded Knee. Note the variety of headgear and equality of clothing. (US National Archives).

9: The End of the Frontier

*In 1893, the Cherekee Outlet, Indian Territory, was opened for settle-
ment. It was the most spectacular of all the 'runs', over 100,000 men
women and children pouring into the rich grasslands on the appointed
day, September 16. (Oklahoma Historical Society).*

ONE April day in 1889, around 60,000 men, women and children poured
out of Kansas to claim the 160 acres of Indian Territory that anyone
crossing the border could legally grab. The land rush to settle the last
Frontier had begun.

Along with the settlers—racing into land given the Indians for ever—
went outlaws, gamblers, merchants, doctors and the rest, and the stampede was so colossal that a town like Guthrie could spring from nothing
to a population of 10,000 in the course of an afternoon.

The last of these rushes occurred in 1911, four years after Oklahoma became a state. That last rush could be claimed as the official ending of the Frontier, but the end of the old West, wild or otherwise, cannot really be given a single date.

By 1911, most ranchers, who for years had regarded sheepmen as the lowest form of life except for their revolting, range-wrecking, stream-befouling 'woollies', and who had never allowed mutton to pass their lips, were actually to be found herding sheep. Cattlemen and sheepmen were at least co-existing in many places, though the last massacre of men and sheep had happened as late as 1909 in Wyoming.

By the end of the century, the day of the gunfighter was almost finished, and the last of the outlaw bands were finding things harder than before. Many outlaws were six feet under ground, locked in state prisons, or going straight, though there was still enough disorder to keep the Texas Rangers, the Arizona Rangers, Pinkerton detectives and lawmen and their posses active. Some wanted men headed for South America, its most notable guests being the likeable leader of the Wild Bunch, Butch Cassidy, and his friend, Harry Longbaugh, the Sundance Kid. They probably died under a hail of bullets in Bolivia in 1911, though there are plenty of people to say that another pair of 'Yanquis' died that day, and Butch's sister has it that the two returned to the States and led blameless lives. If legends are believed hardly an outlaw of note died, even ones whose lifeless corpses were found: they simply disappeared, not even writing their memoirs for Mr Hearst.

The old dynamite days, when outlaws treated trains in the traditional manner, finally ended with the last hold-up of all in 1912, though the plan misfired. Ben Kilpatrick, alias the Tall Texan, and once a star member of the Wild Bunch, was one of the hold-up men, but now he was an ageing gunslinger whose reflexes were getting slow. His companion in crime was a minor character called Nick Grider. They managed to stop the train, but while Grider was keeping the crew covered, the Tall Texan was struck down with an ice mallet, wielded by a guard. Moments later, Grider was shot through the head, and an era had come to an end.

The Indians endured a period of total bleakness from the end of the wars until the 1930s, when, after years of having their culture officially eroded by white teachers, missionaries and administrators, the Roosevelt New Deal allowed them to be Indians again and to recover their pride of race.

Some Indians had already become oil rich, some, especially in Oklahoma, were an essential part of the state. Others showed special skills, most notable the many Mohawks whose fearlessness at great heights still make them ideal skyscraper builders, though many return to their reservations out of season, bearing the white man's gadgets as their ancestors once bore their plunder northwards. But many Indians who have left the reservation, lacking in education, have fallen to the back of the rat race in big cities. At least on a reservation, however bad, the rich, ancient communal life could—and can—be lived. Only now is the Indians' lack of interest in money-making, so perverse in white eyes, being understood more, as is their feeling for the land. The first Americans were the country's first and best conservationists.

Another bleak period for the Indians came in the 1950s when a policy of closing the reservations and allegedly integrating them into the community was instituted. It was a disaster and in at least one case, merely a land grab. Now in the 1970s the fight is on to improve reservations, to get back money and land.

The Vanishing American is vanishing no longer. Charles Russell, quoted at the end of the last chapter, would rejoice at his friends' escape from the valley of the shadow. Yet if the Indians can retain their identity for another century, can survive to live separate but proudly equal alongside the American way of life, it will be a miracle.

As for the West, it can still be found for those who leave the motorways and the beaten tracks and let their imagination roam. But even if most of what is left of it becomes an endless Los Angeles interspersed with national parks, its story could never die, for that story, both myth and fact, is now part of the heritage not only of America, but of the whole world.

Appendix 1: Books for further Reading

All these books are either in print or fairly easy to obtain

Chapters 1 and 2

The Journals of Lewis and Clark. Complete and abridged editions include two single volumes, Bernard de Voto's edition (Boston, 1953: London, 1954) and John Bakeless's (Mentor Books, 1964).

Life in the Far West, by George Frederick Ruxton, edited by Leroy R. Hafen. (University of Oklahoma Press, 1951).

Jim Bridger, by J. Cecil Alter (University of Oklahoma Press, 1962).

Jedediah Smith and the Opening of the West, by Dale Morgan (Indianapolis, 1953: University of Nebraska Press, paperback, 1962).

Chapter 2

Westward Vision, by David Lavender (New York, 1962: Eyre and Spottiswoode Frontier Library, 1965).

The Texas Republic, by William Hogan (University of Oklahoma Press, 1946).

The Gathering of Zion: The Story of the Mormon Trail, by Wallace Stegner (New York, 1964: London, 1966).

The Oregon Trail, Francis Parkman's classic, has been reprinted many times, including a paperback edition in Signet Classics (1961).

Ordeal by Hunger, by George R. Stewart, the grim story of the Donner Party (New York and London, 1936), has ben revised and reprinted, including in a Corgi edition (1964).

Chapter 3

Eldorado, by Bayard Taylor (New York, 1850: New York, 1949, edited by R. G. Cleland, in one volume).

The Big Bonanza, by Dan de Quille. A modern edition of this classic about the Comstock appeared in Eyre and Spottiswoode's Frontier Library (1969).

Klondike, by Pierre Berton. A modern classic (U.S.A. and Canada, 1958: W. H. Allen, 1960).

Chapter 4

The Chisholm Trail, by Wayne Gard (University of Oklahoma Press, 1954).

The American Cowboy, by Joe B. Frantz and Julian E. Choate, (University of Oklahoma Press, 1955). Its apt sub-title is *The Myth and the Reality.*

The Cattle Kings, by Lewis Atherton (Chicago, 1961).

The Log of a Cowboy, the classic (allegedly fictional) cowboy book (Boston, 1903), has run to a number of editions including those by Holiday House (1965) and Ronald Whiting and Wheaton (1966).

Chapter 5

Frontier Justice, by Wayne Gard (University of Oklahoma Press, 1949).
The Texas Rangers, by Walter Prescott Webb (Revised edition, University of Texas Press, 1966).
They Called Him Wild Bill, by Joseph G. Rosa (University of Oklahoma Press, 1964).
Arizona's Dark and Bloody Ground, by Earle R. Forrest (Caxton Printers 1936), the story of the Pleasant Valley War.
Two classics are *The Banditti of the Plains* by A. S. Mercer, a splendidly biassed account of the Johnson County War, and *The Vigilantes of Montana* by Thomas Dimsdale. Both are in the Western Frontier Library (UOP). Nearly every gunfighter has his biographer, but few of this type of book are reliable, unlike articles appearing in specialist publications by State Historical Societies etc.

Chapter 6

The Overland Mail, 1849-69, by Leroy R. Hafen (Cleveland, 1926).
The First Trans-Continental Railroad, by John D. Galloway (New York, 1950).

Chapters 7 and 8

Custer's Luck, by Edgar I. Stewart (Unversity of Oklahoma Press, 1955)
General George Crook, his Autobiography, edited by Martin Schmitt (UOP, 1946).
On the Border with Crook, by John Gregory Bourke, a classic, reprinted by the Rio Grande Press (1962).
The Truth About Geronimo, by Britton Davis (Yale, 1929). Another classic, now available as a Yale paperback.
The Last Days of the Sioux Nation, by Robert M. Utley (Yale, 1963). Also available as a paperback.
Sitting Bull, by Stanley Vestal (Boston, 1932: UOP, 1957).
Crazy Horse, by Mari Sandoz (Hastings House, 1942).
The Fighting Cheyennes, by George Bird Grinnell (New York, 1915: UOP, 1956).
The American Heritage Book of Indians (1961).
Most of the Indian tribes, great and small, have a book or books to themselves in Oklahoma's magnificent *The Civilization of the American Indian Series*.

Chapter 9

A History of Oklahoma, by Grant Foreman (University of Oklahoma Press 1942).
There are many general histories of the West, including some fine pictorial ones. Amongst popular historians whose works are well worth reading are those by Richard Dillon and Paul Wellman, notably the latter's writings on the Indian Wars.

Appendix 2: Some contemporary events

1805. Battle of Trafalgar. Lewis and Clark reach the Pacific.

1808. Peninsular War begins. John Colter's 'Race against Death'.

1815. Battle of Waterloo. First upstream journey from New Orleans to Louisville by a steamer, the **Enterprise**.

1822. The Congress of Verona. The 'To Enterprising Young Men. . .' advertisement appears in the **Missouri Gazette**.

1836. Great Trek of the Boers. Fall of the Alamo.

1843. Sind annexed by Sir Charles Napier. First major party reaches Oregon.

1848. Year of Revolutions in Europe. Gold found in California.

1858. **Great Eastern** launched. Indian Mutiny crushed. First Overland Mail stage reaches Tipton, Missouri, from San Francisco.

1862. Bismarck becomes Prussia's chief minister. Uprising of the Minnesota Sioux.

1864. Fall of Atlanta. Geneva Convention originated. Henry Plummer hanged.

1866. Austro-Prussian War. Start of Red Cloud's War.

1867. Emperor Maximilian shot. Joseph McCoy at Abilene

1869. Suez Canal opened. Union Pacific Railroad opened across America.

1871. Destruction of the Paris Commune. Wild Bill Hickok made Marshal of Abilene.

1874. Disraeli succeeds Gladstone as Prime Minister. Gold found in the Black Hills.

1876. Alexander Bell's first telephone call. Custer's Last Stand. Hickok murdered at Deadwood.

1877. Victoria made Empress of India. Chief Joseph's fighting retreat.

1878. Swan and Edison's first completely successful incandescent light. Lincoln County War.

1881. Pasteur's public anti-anthrax immunisation experiment. Gunfight at the OK Corral.

1886. Daimler's first motor car. End of the Apache Wars.

1890. Forth Bridge opened. End of the Indian Wars.

1902. Boer War ends. Butch Cassidy and the Sundance Kid head for South America.

1907. New Zealand a Dominion. Indian Territory becomes Oklahoma.

1912. The **Titanic** sunk. Last train hold-up in the West.

Acknowledgements

THE generosity shown by Americans towards British of the West is never less than remarkable. So, though the photographs in this book all carry credit lines, the friendly helpfulness of individuals in State Historical Societies, Museums, Libraries etc. towards the author must be specially mentioned.

Pride of place must go to Eugene Decker and Joe Snell of the Kansas State Historical Society and Mrs Katherine Halverson and Mrs Laura Hayes of the Wyoming State Archives and Histo.ical Department. Mrs Halverson has been particularly helpful in showing 'facts' to be myths Mrs Louise Small of the Nebraska State Historical Society and Margaret Lester of the Utah State Historical Society both transformed vague requests into magnificent photographs, and Irene Neasham and the staff of the Wells Fargo Bank History Room in San Francisco lived up to their reputation of being one of the most delightful and helpful groups of people in the business.

James H. Davis of the Denver Public Library, Western History Department, was courtesy itself, as were Jack Haley and June Witt of the University of Oklahoma Western History Collections, the staffs of the Oklahoma and Arizona Historical Societies and J. D. Young of the Custer Battlefield National Monument. Both Union Pacific and Pinkerton's supplied splendid mementoes of their pasts, and major institutions were their usual efficient selves, notably the Library of Congress (Jerry Kearns), the National Archives and the Smithsonian.

In Canada, the Royal Canadian Police were, as always, ready to supply fine pictures of their unique and glorious past.

R.M.
Wimbledon, 1973